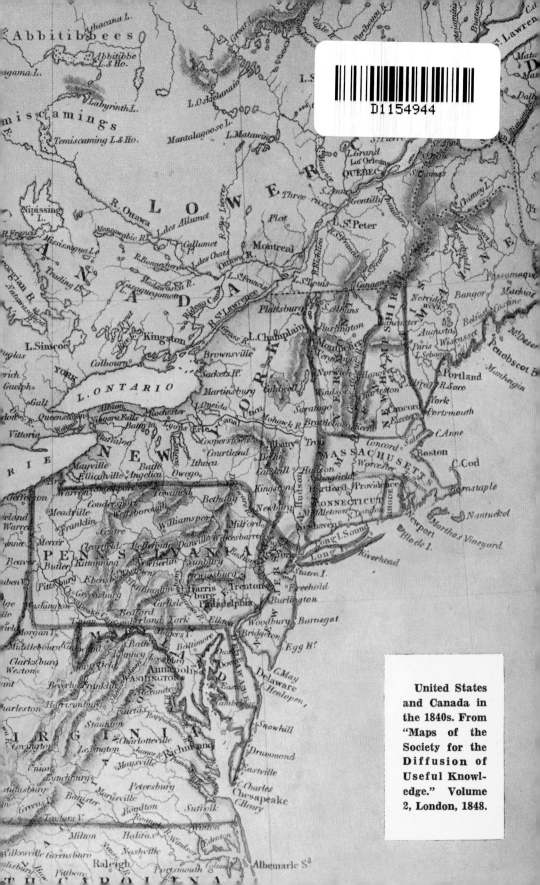

D1154944

JOHN S. WRIGHT

BOOKS BY THE SAME AUTHOR

Author of
SHERMAN: FIGHTING PROPHET
MYTHS AFTER LINCOLN

Co-author with Henry Justin Smith
CHICAGO: THE HISTORY OF ITS REPUTATION

JOHN S. WRIGHT

Prophet of the Prairies

BY

LLOYD LEWIS

ILLUSTRATED

CHICAGO

The Prairie Farmer Publishing Company

1941

From a photograph made presumably in the 1850s or '60s.

John S. Wright

Foreword

I T WAS soon after I returned to Chicago in 1909 and became
publisher of *Prairie Farmer* that I first read of John S.
Wright in the few early volumes I found in *Prairie Farmer's*
library. What I read was enough to whet my curiosity about the
man and his work. A stalwart old pioneer of the city, Ferdinand
Peck, knew him when a boy, and told me that it was hard to understand why an early settler like Wright should have been entirely
forgotten by the city for which he had done so much. Peck would
tell how his own father and Wright had built the third frame
building to go up in the muddy village of Chicago, and how he,
himself, liked to hear Wright and his father, as elderly men,
discuss in their time the glorious future of the city that was to be.
It was something like music, Peck said, to hear Wright sound his
prophesies of what his beloved city was destined to become.

That Wright should have founded *Prairie Farmer* seemed to
me important, but as I listened to Peck, it seemed really less important than many another of Editor Wright's achievements—all
of which had apparently been forgotten. *Prairie Farmer* from its
founding had been set upon a mission of service beyond the field
of agriculture. The successful farming and stock raising that
Wright taught were only to be the material basis necessary for
the broader education and culture that was to make the great
Middle West of today.

Wright had said: "We must first have common schools." He
had built Chicago's first school building at his own expense, and
done more than any other one man to spread common schools
across the frontier—yet there was not a school building named
for him in Chicago.

"He was undoubtedly the father of Chicago's magnificent park
system," wrote my friend H. C. Chatfield-Taylor in his introduction for the biography of Wright we had planned years ago,
"and no park in Chicago today bears his name."

Twenty-five years ago we had begun our research extending
over several years, combing all available sources to glean material for a biography of Wright. It was to be published on *Prairie
Farmer's* 75th anniversary in 1916. Then came the World War

with defense work and the Wright project stood still. We said we would wait until *Prairie Farmer's* centennial in 1941.

It was in 1929 reading the newly published "Chicago: The History of Its Reputation," I discovered that one of its authors, Lloyd Lewis, also appreciated this greatly neglected pioneer reformer. His moving references to Wright's visions determined me. I would write this strange man's biography myself—the complete story of his services and his consecration to the joint cause of Chicago and the surrounding prairie. But events prevented me from doing this and in 1940 I asked Lewis if he remembered John S. Wright. He answered that he had never ceased picking up historical items about the man, and that his curiosity concerning so arresting a figure was endless. The result was that Mr. Lewis and I set out on what proved to be for both of us, a labor of love. Mr. Lewis put aside other biographical works which were to follow his well-known "Sherman: Fighting Prophet." In Illinois, in Washington, D. C., in New York and Boston he has prosecuted the research for this book, and he has written it with his own independence of viewpoint and high standards of scholarship.

It has seemed fitting to me to publish Wright's biography in this year of 1941, the 100th anniversary of his entrance upon the pioneer prairie scene as a reformer, public servant and pioneer prairie editor. My first concern is to see that it is installed in public and university libraries where it will be available to people who want to know whence came our midland civilization and who laid its foundations a century ago.

To me the facts about Wright, as now told, are deeply moving —how in wealth and poverty he gave himself generously to the betterment of pioneer life, preaching the gospel of railroads, of common schools and public parks and playgrounds, of democracy, of better grasses, trees, livestock, roads—a great imagination dealing in practical things. Ridiculed in his own time as a "wild-eyed visionary", a "crazy writin' feller" by the very people whose pockets and minds he enriched, he was, as this book establishes, a seer, a preacher, a prophet far ahead of his day and time.

So it is profound pleasure to me to realize that Mr. Lewis and I now have made this contribution toward saving Wright's memory from passing so undeservedly into the limbo of forgotten men.

December 1, 1941 *Burridge D. Butler*

Contents

Illustrations

JOHN S. WRIGHT

CHAPTER I

"Frontier Town, Lowest Class"

J OHN STEPHEN WRIGHT'S first view of the prairie and of Chicago was on October 28, 1832, while he and his father, "Deacon" Wright, stood at the rail of a lake schooner as it came in from Lake Michigan to anchor near the mouth of the shallow Chicago River—more commonly called "Garlic Creek."

To the boy, at 17, both the frontier village and the sweeping prairie behind it were stirring matters, but to the father who was 49 and who had ridden through the place seventeen years before, Chicago was a squalid sight. It had virtually stood still since the Deacon's casual visit, back in 1815. At that time it had held possibly a dozen cabins which housed French fur hunters, Indians, half-breeds and a minority of Anglo-Saxons who lived off the pelt trade. A few fur traders had lived here back in 1803 when the pig-tailed soldiers of the United States had come to build Fort Dearborn, and now, in 1832, the number of cabins had increased, possibly to thirty.

Two frame buildings had been built during the summer, but in general Chicago was merely an old, static, frontier hamlet—a backwash of civilization. Nobody could be sure whether the population was 150, or 100 or less, so rapidly did the fur hunters come and go. The company of soldiers in the fort had little to do except talk about their predecessors who had been killed in the famous frontier incident, "The Fort Dearborn Massacre" in 1812.

The few immigrants who had come through late this

summer and autumn had been pointed toward more promising regions farther inland, and the Wrights, father and
son, were headed for Galena, reputedly the future metropolis of the West, standing on the Mississippi River some
200 miles to the northwest.

What irked Deacon Wright was that he and his son
must stop in Chicago for days, perhaps weeks, before
starting for Galena. There had been a mistake about the
shipment of merchandise they were bringing to sell. Only
a portion of their goods had come with them on the
schooner, the rest had missed the boat at Buffalo and now
they must wait till it came on the next schooner.

The Wright boy was glad to be done, for a time, with
traveling. It had been three weeks since they had left
Massachusetts, riding the first few miles behind a primitive locomotive, then a long stretch on one of the creaking
arks that crept along the Erie Canal, and finally the lake
schooner trip from Buffalo to Chicago—the port that happened to afford the shortest overland route to Galena.

Deck hands told passengers not to judge the new country by the swampy lands close to the fur depot. Out there,
behind and beyond, was the most fertile soil this side of
the Nile Valley, the prairie running from Northern Indiana, across Northern and Central Illinois to jump the
great river and roll on across the lands of the Iowa Indians.
It was late autumn now. Wait till spring, when it was a
carpet of flowers—all kinds of flowers in all kinds of colors
—an ocean of blossoms! Wait till you hear the trappers
talk about those flowers!

Between the patches of scrub oaks that lined the sand
dunes along Lake Michigan's edge, young Wright glimpsed
the prairie—a great grassy sea. Indeed, the little log town,
the sand dunes and the trees seemed to stand on an atoll
between *two* seas—one of blue water, one of brown grass.
The same wind made waves in them both, the only striking

difference being the presence of little islands of trees here and there across the vast level expanse of the prairie.

From sailors, a boy could learn that it was the prairie fires that had made the land so bare. Indians started fires in the spring to burn off the dry, dead grass and to hurry on the tender green shoots upon which their ponies fed. They also spread fires in the fall to corner their game.

Men who coursed the prairie said not ten per cent of it was wooded. Those little islands of standing timber were on the east side of streams. The water had saved them from the long lines of fire that moved east across the huge meadow on the prevailing western winds.

As rowboats took the passengers and their boxes ashore, the Wrights saw the inhabitants more clearly. Everybody had come down to the water's edge. Schooners came infrequently to this "frontier town of the lowest class," as a literary traveler had called it. On the banks lounged U. S. soldiers, but the tone of the place was still set, as it had been in 1815, by Frenchmen and Indians and by Frenchmen crossed with Indians.

The daily life of the depot was lived by blanketed red men gambling with fur-clad trappers in the dooryards, by hunters taking their last carousals in the taverns before leaving for the annual harvest of skins along northern waters, by voyageurs fighting or laughing with the Hoosier hucksters who brought fruit, vegetables or bacon up from the rich Wabash River country 150 miles to the southeast.

"The whites seemed to be more pagan than the reds," observed Charles Joseph Latrobe, a traveler. He saw "horse-stealers and horse-dealers, rogues of every description ... sharpers of every degree ... squaws, papooses ... the interior of the village a chaos of mud, rubbish and confusion ... in the hotels an appalling confusion of filth and racket ... horse races on the sward outside the village daily

... Indians in gaudy attire ... fighting, knives raised, then quieted by good-natured Indians."

All this was depressing to the Deacon, entrancing to his son, as they came rolling up to town in a wagon from the sands of the shore.

Inquiring as to which of the taverns might be least offensive, the Deacon was directed to one that stood on the opposite side of the meandering river's South Branch. A ferry would be there to take them over. But when their wagon had creaked up to the river, no ferry was in sight. They waited, and soon there approached a large and effusive Frenchman who touched his hat and inquired, "You going to stop here?"

"Yes," said Deacon Wright, "we had heard that the hotel was on the other side."

The Frenchman pointed to a log house standing near at hand and on their side of the river. Above its door was a sign, "Sauganash Tavern."

"This is my house," screamed the Chicagoan. "Me keep tavern like hell; play de fiddle like damnation; you no stop with me?"

Laughing, Deacon Wright and his son moved in. They had met, in Mark Beaubien, a character, fashioned as if by the gods of fiction for the amusement of a 17-year-old boy.

This tavern, standing at what was later to be Lake and Market streets, was kept, indeed, as Beaubien had described. Drunkards bellowed in it, civilized guests complained, Indians snoozed on the threshold, tipsy loafers roared with laughter as the host played his fiddle and sang songs. Gamblers put up their money on coming horse races or wolf hunts. Mrs. Beaubien screeched at the half-breed hired girls who ran between stove and dinner table with dishes slopping.

Upstairs in a loft, reached by a ladder, fifty men could

sleep if closely packed on the floor. Beaubien covered the first comers with blankets, then covertly slipped the coverings from the snoring men to give to newcomers as they arrived. It was a common saying in Chicago that Mark had been known to make two pairs of blankets cover forty men in a single night.

If one of the shivering guests who backed down the ladder in the morning growled about the lack of covering, Mark would laugh and rebate half the bill. In time the Wrights learned that the reason the ferry had not been ready to transport them across the river to a rival hotel was because Mark Beaubien, himself, was the ferryman.

Tales of similar cleverness were told of Mark's brother, Jean Baptiste Beaubien, agent of a fur company, colonel of the militia company, and one of the hamlet's early settlers. Once, back in 1825, he had been hired to help United States troops work 700 cattle across the Chicago River on the way from Southern Illinois to Green Bay, and, since his brother's family was out of beef, Colonel Jean had adroitly maneuvered one of the fattest steers into drowning.

Jean was more restrained than his brother and in time would have only nineteen children, whereas Mark, by successive marriages, had twenty-three.

With his merchandise stored, and his son housed at the "Sauganash" where Mrs. Beaubien gave him loud assurances that the boy would be safe, Deacon Wright bought a horse and struck off inland exploring. So long as he had to wait in the town, he might as well look around. Immigration was said to be trickling into the Fox River Valley out to the northwest on the way to Galena. It might be that there a man could find a better place for a store than in the already popular city on the Mississippi.

Scarcely had the father disappeared over the damp western horizon before young John S. Wright was all over the post, scouring the contents of the log stores, noting what merchandise was selling and at what prices, studying travelers, finding out what made them come to Chicago.

Then, waiving the fact that, as a minor, he had no legal authority to make contracts or transact business, he rented a vacant log cabin of Mark Beaubien, at the southeast corner of Lake and Market streets, and, unpacking his father's boxes, opened a store.

Ten days had not passed since his father's departure before the boy, making friends with another young Easterner, Philo Carpenter, went out with him onto the prairie west of the settlement and held the chain while a surveyor measured them off a quarter section of land apiece. Taking it in his father's name the boy guaranteed to pay the pre-emption price of $1.25 an acre.

What his father would say, the boy didn't know. Perhaps the answer was already forecast in the laughter the older inhabitants of the village set up when anyone, let alone a mere boy, bought swamp lands around the place. It was crazy speculation, that was all.

Southern Illinois was the place to go if you wanted land—down there rivers could carry you to St. Louis or Cincinnati with your produce. So rapidly had immigrants poured from Kentucky into the southern half of the State that Illinois as a whole had tripled its population in the past ten years, but Chicago and northern Illinois still slumbered on.

Elsewhere in the twenty-five States of the Union this November crowds were cheering the victory of Andy Jackson over Henry Clay in the presidential elections, or quarreling over the attempt of South Carolinians to declare a Federal tariff law null and void—an issue that endangered the Union itself. But in the trading post of Chicago, the talk was of pelts and grog and wolf hunts.

A few citizens had half-heartedly surveyed the village and laid off some streets, but nothing more had been done.

From an early print in the library of the Chicago Historical Society.

South Water Street, Chicago, on the Chicago River in 1834.

Two frame buildings had gone up the past summer. There had been talk of a harbor that would turn the city into a port, but that, too, had subsided.

What young Wright had seen, as his father had not, and as the whole town had not—was that here was the place for a great city. To him it was all perfectly plain: with land so rich and cheap it was inevitable that the prairie must soon be filled with farmers; if the fur traders of the Northwest brought their pelts to Chicago, then the farmers must do the same.

Five years before, Congress had authorized Illinois to build a canal from Lake Michigan to the Illinois River, and thus, to the Mississippi. Trade from the interior would, when this canal was built, come to Chicago seeking ships. This made it certain that a harbor would some day be dug at the river's mouth.

Into the village he saw the "prairie schooners" roll, huge Conestogas, Pennsylvania mountain wagons, curved at each end like Roman galleys, lurching through the mud while drivers cracked long whips over the backs of eight or ten yoke of oxen. These were the huckster wagons of the Hoosiers from the banks of the Wabash, and the sound of their little bells tinkling on the ox yokes, the sight of peaches and apples dangling on thongs at the wagon ends as advertisements, and the cries of the drivers, "Whoa-haw-gee" to the cattle, and "Apples! Peaches! Butter! Lard! Ham! Dry Fruit! Green Fruit!" brought the housewives hurrying to buy and the small boys to steal.

At night the glow of the Hoosiers' bivouac fires along Michigan Avenue, and the fragrance of frying bacon and corn dodgers kept a fringe of town boys hovering like mosquitoes.

Wright saw that if these peddlers found it profitable to come now 100 miles over roads that were little better than Indian trails, the farm trade into Chicago must prove enormous in the populous years of the future.

Nature, in his mind, had decreed Chicago's future.

In a particular field he saw the future as the Hoosiers sketched it. This, he described years later when telling how, while boarding with "that whole-souled friend of mine and natural gentleman, Mark Beaubien," he had seen Indiana drovers arrive with razor-back hogs, "the breed more famous for the time they could make than for the lard they could yield. The bipeds staid a week or two to kill and pack the quadrupeds, and it was my privilege to have the former for fellow-boarders. They were never too busy with the killing and never wasted time with washing, to keep them behind at mealtimes.

"Mrs. Beaubien, noble woman that she was and Christian mother who corrected many of my New England anti-Catholic notions, tried her best to get some of the slap-jacks to me, but the hog-killers were so on the alert that the two weeks fighting for my living impressed upon my memory pretty effectually the early days of Chicago's pork-packing."

Within a few days John Stephen's father came riding back into town waving a piece of paper which indicated that on his trip he, too, had seen that Chicago, not the Fox River valley nor Galena, was the place for them to locate. He said he had ridden to the Fox River, followed it downstream thirty miles, then cut back toward Chicago, stopping overnight with a Mr. Searcy on the prairie. During the evening's talk, Searcy had offered to take $100 for a lot, 80 by 150 feet, on Chicago's Lake Street near Clark. This the elder Wright had bought.

He was pleased, but not surprised, that his son should have opened a store. He noted that the goods were going at prices 100 to 150 per cent above what they had cost in New York. But it was a different matter to have the boy better him in the purchase of real estate, as witness the quarter section of land which John Stephen had secured for him, not more than two miles from the lakefront.

Noting on his travels the land which must some day be tributary to Chicago, he had bought 150 feet frontage in the mudtown, but his son had gone in for 160 acres!

The die was cast, and within a few days Deacon Wright set off for Massachusetts to tell the rest of his family the news—they were all coming to Chicago to live. By hurrying he could get home before winter fell, and in the spring he would be back to rejoin his boy. It would be risky to leave one so young as John Stephen in charge of a store in the wild frontier town for so many months. But the Deacon knew his son.

A pioneer punka; drawing sent to *The Prairie Farmer* (published November, 1851) by a reader, Geo. K. Aydelott, Mead county, Kentucky, with his description of his "Fly Machine"—"with very little motion of the chair the operator can fan the table, rock the child and talk to his wife all at the same time."

CHAPTER II

The Child Prodigy

IT WAS in the home of her father, Stephen Dewey, 2nd, at Sheffield, Massachusetts, that Huldah Dewey had been married on September 26, 1814. It was there that her first child, John Stephen Wright, was born on July 16, 1815. One of seven sisters, she was an "old maid," in the common view of the time, when she had married, and the love of family was strong in her. According to a friend, many of "the rare endowments of mind and heart" which graced her, had come from growing up "in her New England home in an atmosphere of the purest Christian love and refinement."

Education in that home had been held in high esteem even for New England. Huldah, herself, had taught school for many years previous to her marriage. Her brother Chester, two years her senior, had been, since his twenty-sixth year, a full-fledged professor of mathematics and natural philosophy at Williams College. In 1814, he already was well on his way to the national fame which was to come to him as an educator. Between this brother and herself there were not only the bonds of exceptionally strong family affection but of ethical ideals. Both were marked by observers as having "a great deal of zeal and energy, *pro publico bono*."

Considering the closeness of their spirits, it must have been with the consent of Chester that Huldah married John Wright, a storekeeper of Sheffield. It was not a match of young and heedless love, for John Wright was,

as things went in the early 19th century, a middle-aged
man, almost thirty-one, at the time. Like Huldah he came
of many generations of New England stock, having been
born in Colchester, Connecticut, November 25, 1783, to
John and Lucy Wright. As a young man he had moved
to Sheffield, where he set up as a merchant. Religion and
public education had interested him, too, and he, as
"Deacon" Wright, fit naturally into the atmosphere of
the Dewey family.

Soon after his marriage, John Wright's health failed
and it was decided that he must try and regain it by a
trip that would take him into the open air. In 1815 he set
off on horseback for the Far West and returned in 1816
much improved. On July 16, 1815, either before his departure or soon thereafter, his wife had given birth to a
son in her father's house, naming him after his two grand-
fathers, John and Stephen. Other sons followed at two-
year intervals: Timothy on April 16, 1817; Walter on May
30, 1819; and Edward on October 5, 1821. But it was upon
the eldest that the hopes of the family were built.

While there might have been exaggeration in the story
that John Stephen was reading Greek at three, there was
no question about his mother having carried him far into
arithmetic, grammar and geography by the time he was
seven.

Orderly, exact, a notable housekeeper, Mrs. Wright
was deeply religious and had made up her mind early
that this eldest son should be a minister. In later years
John Stephen would tell about the strictness with which
Sunday had been observed across his boyhood. The Lord's
Day began on Saturday when the sun went down, and for
twenty-four hours thereafter no child could laugh, sing
or run. The little Wrights sat for interminable hours in
an old meeting-house, went home to a cold dinner, and
then awaited the tantalizingly slow droop of the sun to-

ward the Western hills. When its upper rim had disappeared, they could run and roar once more with Bose, John Stephen's dog.

It was when John Stephen was seven that his mother felt herself unequipped to educate him further. The family moved to Williamstown so that her brother, the professor, might take over the supervision of this work. Selling his store in Sheffield, Deacon Wright opened another in Williamstown and settled down to let his four little boys grow up in their uncle's shadow.

Chester Dewey promptly sent one of his prize students, named Willey, to live in the Wright home and tutor the children. Surveying his charges, John Stephen seven, Timothy five, Walter three and Edward one, Willey put the eldest to studying Latin and kept that as his chief study for the next four years. At ten John Stephen was far enough along to go to Williams College to recite Greek and other subjects to more advanced instructors, one of them a Mr. Bradley, and another a Mr. Hopkins. Years later, when Hopkins, the tutor, was Professor Mark Hopkins, one of the great names in American higher education, he said that John Stephen Wright's mind was one of the brightest ever to come under his instruction.(1)

By the time he was twelve, the boy was studying algebra, Greek, Latin and Euclid in an academy which had sprung up near the college, and at fourteen he was sent to his uncle Chester's private school, the Berkshire Gymnasium, which the professor's father-in-law had built for him.

Over the boy the uncle brooded with pride. Here was the prodigy of the family. And never did he ever chide the boy except for playing chess instead of outdoor games in recreation time.

Although John Stephen was intended for an educa-

(1) In Memoriam: John S. Wright by Augustine W. Wright.

tional and clerical career, there were practical matters to be considered. His father was not prospering sufficiently to keep his son at boarding school, so John Stephen added bookkeeping to his studies. After 1830, when he was fifteen, he went home for six months to handle his father's accounts and to receive an interest in the store. With the profits from this, he returned for another year of schooling at the Berkshire Gymnasium.

Education had been easy for the boy, and now, although his father's store was a small one, business was easy, too—also it was exciting. John Stephen began to wonder if he wanted to be a preacher, after all. It would be a great blow to his mother even to discuss, now, a change in plans.

However, a family calamity came early in 1832 to assist the boy in his gropings. His father discovered that he could no longer afford to give his children the education that the Dewey tradition demanded. There were six children now, John Stephen, soon to be seventeen, Timothy fifteen, Walter thirteen, Anne Eliza eight, Edward six (the first Edward had died seven years before), and Frances Sarah five. Still another child, Lucia Sophia, had died three years earlier at the age of two.

The Deacon felt he must go West—emigrate to the Far West, where, he understood, better opportunities for himself and his family existed. It would be a wrench to pull up roots as deep as the Wrights' and the Deweys' and go into the wilderness where there were no colleges, no old elm-shaded rows of white cottages, none of the comforts and peace of the ancient New England civilization.

What was probably John Stephen's first hint of this decision of his father's came when the boy, at school, went to his uncle, Professor Dewey, to announce his own wish to be a merchant instead of a preacher. He explained that he could have a "greater opportunity for rising" in the new field and that he expected to enter a store in New York where his father's brother, Amasa, lived.

"You'll do no such thing," said Professor Dewey, "your father intends to take you to the Far West and let you make a man of yourself, and that's my own advice as the best way to bring you out."

Later the boy described his satisfaction as "intense" at being thus released from the ministerial future by the uncle who had been his guide for as long as he could remember, and whose opinion he knew to be most influential with his mother. Within a few weeks he went home to prepare for the trip and, doubtless to give her assurance that his soul would be safe in the wilderness among pagan Indians, strange French Catholics and other influences traditionally regarded as hostile by Puritan New Englanders, he joined the Congregational Church—the date being the first Sunday in June of that year, 1832.

His father, as a devoutly religious man, was prepared to spread Protestant Christianity on the frontier when they should arrive, but he had great confidence, as had Professor Dewey, that the boy could take care of himself and his traditions in any situation. He allowed John Stephen to go on alone to New York, where supplies for the Western venture were to be bought. The Deacon followed a little later to find his brother Amasa and family still astonished at the country boy's capability in finding them in the great city, and in the ease with which he was "seeing" it.

He had already told them that he couldn't think of leaving for the West without having seen New York and that he "hoped to help build a great city out there."

Where that city would be was highly vague in his mind since his father had as yet not decided on what section of the Western wilderness they would visit. Deacon Wright had seen much of it, seventeen years before, when he had taken his trip by horse across Ohio, Indiana and Illinois to the Mississippi River, thence by steamboat to New Orleans. Since then Indiana and Illinois had changed from territories to States, and there was much talk of settlers taking up rich lands in the Territory of Michigan which sprawled across forests and lakes, great and small, all the way from Detroit to the Canadian line just north of the headwaters of the Mississippi.

When the Indians should be moved off the huge Northwest, great cities might start anywhere, everywhere. No one could be sure where the big opportunities would come, with so many thousands of square miles of rich, black soil available at $1.25 an acre. To thrifty Yankees who had scrabbled a meager living from the stony fields of New England, this "Congress land" of the Far West seemed a bargain indeed, and the spirit of emigration was fermenting all along the Atlantic seaboard.

From Pennsylvania and the Middle Atlantic States the way to the new lands was by wagon over trails (preferably the National Road) across Ohio and Indiana, or from Pittsburgh down the Ohio River to Cincinnati in steamboats which were jocosely called "floating volcanoes." From New England the trip was quicker and easier by way of the Erie Canal from Albany to Buffalo and from there by schooner to Detroit where wagons could be taken or the trip continued around through Lakes Huron and Michigan.

For the Wrights, living as they did at Williamstown, close to Albany, the water route was the better, at least to Buffalo, where they could make up their minds as to their destination. That much decided, the elder Wright invested between $5,000 and $6,000 in the kind of merchandise which he expected to sell most readily on the frontier, and ordered it shipped to Buffalo where he and his son would meet it early in October.

There were farewells, promises of a speedy return with news of what they found in the wilderness, and they were off. For 16 miles of the journey they traveled on the newly finished Mohawk and Hudson Railroad, at the dazzling pace of six and a half miles an hour. In Buffalo they found a schooner preparing for the long voyage—almost three weeks—to the incipient ports that had arisen at the southern end of Lake Michigan, and, basing his judgment on what he already knew and what he could learn, the elder Wright booked passage for the full trip.

Seventeen years before he had been much impressed with the fertility of Northern Illinois and within recent weeks the news had come that the United States Army had cleaned out the last of the Indian war makers in that region.

That summer of '32 Chief Black Hawk had started a revolt that had sent the scattering white settlers flying to the nearest blockhouses. With the ensuing arrival of the Regulars accompanied by war correspondents, publicity had come to a sharp focus upon that flat and fertile expanse of land which the earlier French had called the Grand Prairie. Black Hawk had been overthrown in August and it was now safe for homeseekers to traverse the great sea of grass and select the claims which could be entered as soon as a promised treaty with the Indians could be made.

Deacon Wright, asking questions of lake sailors, of travelers, of all possible authorities in Buffalo, had finally decided on Galena, Illinois, as his destination.

When the Deacon came home to his wife and his other children late in the year, he was full of enthusiasm for the new location, Chicago, and although it would be too soon, everything considered, to take the whole family West the next spring, he himself, would go back as soon as the Great Lakes schooners started to run, build a home and be ready for Huldah and the younger children to come out in '34.

The mother wondered about her son, so young, so scholarly, alone in the wild frontier post as the winter of 1832-33 passed.

As a matter of fact the youth was behaving most circumspectly. To avoid the hubbub and revelry at the Sauganash Tavern, he moved his bed to the store and slept under the counter. During the day, when there were no customers, he stood in the door practising with firearms upon the snow-birds and prairie chickens, and of evenings he sat by the fireplace reading the Greek classics, while across the snowy flats came the rollicking mirth of Mark Beaubien's fiddle and the boat songs of voyageurs.

When the original stock of merchandise had run out, the boy had begun trading in firearms. As the operator of a gunnery, he soon became a crack marksman, never, however, being drawn into the riotous chases in which carousing riders followed dogs after prairie wolves, deer and bear, across the marshes north of the river.

Instead, he went to the rudimentary religious services which Captain Seth Johnson, commander of the garrison, held at the fort on Sundays, or to the prayer meetings which the Reverend Jesse Walker, a Methodist circuit rider, conducted when at home in an old log house which he and his family used for parsonage, parlor, bedroom, kitchen and meeting house. Sunday School was held in this cabin with young Wright acting as librarian, carrying to and from each session, the whole library wrapped in a handkerchief. These few books, discarded by some Eastern Sunday School, had been sent out to the Western heathen, who in the person of French and half-breed urchins sat on split log benches waving their best moccasins in the face of the Wright boy who read them the new and strange gospels.

That February of 1833, young Wright helped raise the third frame building in the hamlet—the store of P. F. W. Peck at the southeast corner of South Water and LaSalle Streets—and soon was helping move the Sunday School into its loft.

The winter was passing. Wild geese began to drop down from the north and rest inside the sand bar outside the river's mouth. An immigrant or two came splashing in from the south—advance guard of the Eastern rush that would soon be arriving. Then, one day, the boy looked up from his counter and saw his father standing in the door. Their greetings over and news of home all told, the Deacon looked around. His jaw dropped. Those guns! Nothing but guns, and ramrods, and powder horns. Had his son turned into a sporting character?

Saying nothing the Deacon went across town to that first of the merchants, George W. Dole, and asked, straight out, how had his son been behaving.

"Never you fear for John," said Dole. "The boys have tried their best to get him into our frolics, but he was no go."(2)

(2) Ibid.

EDUCATIONAL.

Title heading for the Educational Department used by Wright in *The Prairie Farmer* during the 1850s.

ILLINOIS
in 1837.
with proposed improvements.

SCALE OF MILES.

EXPLANATION.
COUNTY TOWNS ●
CANALS
RAIL ROADS
STAGE DO.
COMMON DO.

CHAPTER III

Boy Starts "Boom"

DEACON WRIGHT had come back to Chicago intending to buy as much land as he could at the public auction of a section of school land to be held that spring. His son pressed him to buy without hesitation, but when the time came the Deacon was, as John S. later wrote, "over-cautious . . . too fearful of advancing prices by seeking purchases" and to the boy's bitter disappointment, got only "about $1,000 worth, six lots and two blocks." The whole section had gone for less than $39,000, a sum ridiculously large in the minds of the old inhabitants, ridiculously small in the eyes of the young Greek scholar.

Deacon Wright's imagination was still that of a village tradesman in New England. It was also that of a Puritan, and he was pained by the lack of any adequate religious life on the frontier. When he heard that Captain Johnson and his soldiers were to be transferred, he described himself as "almost ready to despair," fearing that "the troops coming in would all be utterly careless about religion." The more he saw of the drinking and the gambling the more he wrote East praying for the arrival of a regular resident clergyman.

It was on Monday, May 12, that his prayers were answered, for a vessel sailing down from the north with the new garrison, brought along, as chaplain, a full-fledged Presbyterian preacher, the Reverend Jeremiah Porter, who had been urged by the Home Mission Society of Boston to explore the needs of the bawdy trading posts on

Lake Michigan's rim. Noting how quickly the Reverend Porter cleaned out the carpenter shop at the fort, installed pews and commenced preaching, Deacon Wright wept for joy. The new minister, looking over his new parish, noted, as "the first dreadful spectacle that met my eyes," a group of Indians "sitting on the ground before a miserable French dram house playing cards, and as many trifling white men standing around to witness the game." Immediately he resolved to fight the devil here on his own ground with double blasts of righteousness, and so he inaugurated church services at the fort on Sunday mornings and in the Reverend Walker's log cabins in the afternoons. On June 28, when he had the First Presbyterian Church organized, Deacon Wright was one of the elders. Of the twenty-five odd members all but one were Congregationalists, but Presbyterianism was sufficiently near to that faith to make the transfer easy, especially under frontier conditions.

Nine days later Porter was outraged to find almost nobody but women at his services, "the men being away watching a boat unload in the harbor . . . a wanton abuse of the holy day by many who sin against clear light and abuse divine compassion and love." The men, however, encouraged the pastor to hope for the erection of a church building, and a lot was bought at the southwest corner of Lake and Clark, "a lonely spot, almost inaccessible on account of the surrounding sloughs and bogs."

The Wrights, father and son, also had their hands in the organization of the first attempt to educate the children of the post, most of them French and Indians.

In June, when the Wrights were building their new store on the Searcy lot, east of Clark and north of Lake, a Miss Eliza Chappel arrived from Mackinaw, Michigan, announcing that she was a schoolteacher and would like to set up in Chicago the coming autumn. The Wrights told her that as soon as they had their new building ready they would be quitting the old log store which young John had rented from Beaubien, and that she might use this for a schoolhouse. By September they were out and she took over, cutting the interior into two rooms, one for herself and the other for a schoolroom for twenty pupils.

Since the Wrights' new store building was so far from the town's one business street, Water, the scoffing inhabitants nicknamed it "The Prairie Store" and predicted financial disaster, but the builders, particularly John S., were sure that the city would grow out to it.

What filled John S. with unlimited confidence was the news, that summer, that there was hope of a harbor, after all. An army engineer by the name of Jefferson Davis, had persuaded the Government that Chicago, rather than other sites on the lake front, was the place for a port, and a sum of $25,000 was to be appropriated to clear the river's mouth and erect a pier.

Where Chicago had added a dozen buildings and around some twenty new residents in 1832, now in '33 it built forty-three buildings and increased its total population to some 300—some 250 of them reasonably permanent. At least that was what young Wright made it when, to satisfy himself, he took a census. Although only 18 that July, he was in August one of the leaders in pushing the incorporation of Chicago as a town.

Although immigration arrived at what was, to him, a ridiculously slow pace, there were promising signs. The mail from the East, arriving in the saddlebags of a Frenchman who had contracted to bring it from Niles, Michigan, grew so heavy in the latter half of the year that the postman had to walk so the horse could carry the heavy sacks. This meant that settlers were taking up claims all around Chicago. Young Wright saw them coming in from thirty to seventy miles to ask Postmaster Hogan for letters. And around Chicago at night burned the campfires of farmers who slept beside their wagons after a day of trading.

In September came the event, which, to John S. Wright's mind, should have made the blindest of observers see the limitless future of Northern Illinois—the great treaty with the Indians. To meet the white officials came tribesmen for hundreds of miles—Pottawatomies, with some smaller groups of Chippewas and Ottawas, streaming in along the deeply cut and ancient trail from Ypsilanti through White Pigeon Prairie, past South Bend, past La Porte Prairie, past Michigan City, and on past the large camp a group of Pottawatomies kept on the Calumet River close to Chicago.

From all over the surrounding country white men had come to see the spectacle, one of them being a 28-year-old clergyman-educator, Jonathan Baldwin Turner, who like Wright had been born in Massachusetts.

While attending Yale in 1827 Turner, with six other students, had stood under the stars one night to vow that, when their college work was done, they would carry "religion and learning" into the wilderness of the West. He had been given his diploma ahead of his class in 1833 so that he might fill a vacant post on the faculty of Illinois College at Jacksonville, Illinois.

A farm boy who had resolutely put himself through college by teaching in rural schools, a fiery temperance advocate, a born reformer, Turner had shown his traits dramatically in the summer of 1833 when he had refused to flee Jacksonville as the cholera struck, and had stayed, dosing the sick, burying the dead and praying to God.

With the lifting of the pestilence late in August he had taken a horseback vacation and arrived in the log town of Chicago to write his sweetheart back East, "On the lake shore were assembled about 8,000 Indians, decorated with paint and wampum, armed with rifles, tomahawks, bows and arrows, war-clubs, scalping-knives, etc. Their squaws were armed with papooses on their backs."

The day after the Indians had formally sold their lands and agreed to be sent to what they were assured were better hunting grounds west of the Mississippi, Turner told how "the place was filled with drunken Indians, in all stages of helplessness, and all wanting to fight." Old settlers told their wives and the tenderfeet visitors that everything was safe; there were two companies of soldiers in the fort; but there were extra bars on the doors that night in the scattered cabins of the town. Turner saw the squaws gather about the fiercest of the drunken red males, "throw them down. . . . Three heavy squaws were sometimes sitting on one squirming, yelling Indian."[1]

Turner observed how the land which was bought from the Indians for "three cents per acre" was sold next day to the whites for "100 per squire." He and two friends from Jacksonville laughed about the folly of such a rise in values. "We bantered each other to buy, for there was never a more unpromising location for a city than the low, marshy ground of Chicago. We bought one squire of land." The property stood at the southeast corner of Randolph and Dearborn, and later the friends felt fortunate to sell it for $10,000. Turner lived to see it worth millions.

With the signing of the Indian treaty, land to the supposed amount of 5,000,000 acres was ready; everything was ready but the immigrants. When Chicagoans, like Deacon Wright, went East that autumn, and boasted that they had actually paid as high as from $60 to $100 for a lot in the damp settlement, there was shaking of heads. Scoffers admitted that the rich, black earth out there might be a bargain at $1.25 per acre, but why buy town lots? Anyway why go so far into the wilderness? There were still thousands of acres of unsold land in Michigan, and for $200 a

(1) Jonathan Baldwin Turner, by Mary Turner Carriel, 1911.

man could get 160 acres there, much nearer civilization.

But the news of the Indian treaty, of the proposed Illinois and Michigan Canal's terminus at Chicago, and of the digging of a harbor at the river's mouth was spreading. By the spring of 1834, when Deacon Wright brought his wife and five of their children, bag and baggage, to Chicago to live, the rush was on.

Where only eleven steamboats had plied the Great Lakes in 1833, eighteen were busy in 1834. Wagons came rolling along the sand dunes from Michigan City to Chicago, at the rate of six miles a day; stages from Niles broke down in the awful mud of the roads inland, and immigrants flounced and floundered up to their knees in mire while stage drivers heaved on rails and whipped horses to get their broken-axled wagons to firmer ground.

To Huldah Dewey Wright, it was her first view of her son in seventeen months. That the boy had been so active in church matters was a joy to her. He had, in his father's absence that winter, taken an active part in the building of the First Presbyterian Church which had risen in the sloughs—to be exact, on an alley, already called Clark Street, in the rear of what was later the Sherman House. It was dedicated on January 4, 1834, with the thermometer hovering around 24 below, and the winds howling.

Accustomed as they were to the precocity of their eldest son, the Deacon and Huldah Wright must have been amazed, upon their arrival in the spring of '34, to find that after an exchange of letters with his wealthy uncle Amasa, back in Brooklyn, he had become his uncle's representative, and, as he thought, partner.

To convince the older man that Chicago property was little short of a gold mine, he had written descriptions and had drawn for him a map of the town. When he brought his uncle to the point of consenting to a purchase, the boy began working on a Lieutenant Jamison of the

U. S. Army to sell a corner lot bordering on the river.

In time he won the lieutenant over, and on March 11 wrote his uncle: "Last Friday I bought it of him for $3,500, an enormous sum, half of it to be paid on the first of June, 1834, and the other half on the first of December, 1834. There is a lawyer now drawing a writing in reference to the bargain, in which he (Mr. Jamison) binds himself to give a deed of the lot upon payment of the first half, ($1,750). It is ready to be signed tomorrow. This may seem to you to be an enormous sum for a lot (80 ft. by 150 ft.) in Chicago, and I think father would not give half that sum for it. But his ideas do not keep up with property in Chicago. I am sure that lot will in less than three months fetch $5,000. What makes me think so is this: There are a great many merchants coming into Chicago this summer. There are but two or three water lots that can be bought at any price. All the business is at present done on this (Water) street. Now merchants coming in are not going on to the back streets to do business as long as they can get a building spot on Water street, for twice what its real value is. Lots have not yet got to near their full value. That one I bought will within five years be worth three, and I think I may say five times what I paid for it. Chicago will within that time be as large as Detroit is now, and real estate will be worth as much. A small lot there 50 x 60 feet (I think it was) was sold a few weeks since for $10,000 and why should not business lots be worth as much here as there? These are the reasons that made me purchase that lot, and that make me think it was a good bargain. I do not suppose I could get what I paid for it back now, but I can in less than three months."

Hard on the heels of this letter went another, signed the next day, March 12, revealing to the rich man in Brooklyn how fast his nephew was working:

"Last evening I made another bargain for 90½ acres for which I am to pay $3,500. . . . Mr. Noble gives me a quit claim and warranty deed . . . they will be signed tomorrow. I gave him a draft on you (which I hope you will accept) . . . and gave notes in my own name for the remainder. . . . He does not require any endorsers, not anything for security of payment, except the notes. This I think pretty lenient in him, and shows he has some confidence in me. I have not writings from father which would bind him (father) to any bargains I make. I ought to have had some, but I did not think I should so soon be purchasing real estate. . . . If you do not feel secure, I can give you endorsers, for a number of good, substantial men in this place have offered of their own accord to sign for me if I wish it. So you see I am not without friends, if I am here alone."(²)

Five days later the boy bought another corner lot for $12,000 on his own account, borrowing $17 from his father's store and $283 from friends for the down payment of $300. By July 1 he had sold it, turning the $300 into $1,900. This was the first money he had ever made and he opened a set of books for himself as a merchant of real estate.

While there had been some increase in the price of Chicago real estate prior to young Wright's entrance upon the field, he, in the opinion of the Reverend Jeremiah Porter, "was the first to give an impetus to the high price of town lots." Porter, a close observer of the town's material as well as spiritual doings, and exceedingly intimate with the Wright family, declared that the purchase with which John Stephen touched off the fireworks was that of a corner lot on South Water and Dearborn for $1,500 late in 1834. Earlier in the year it had changed hands at $500. Porter noted that "many were astonished at the audacity

(2) Chicago, Past, Present, Future, by John S. Wright, 1870.

of the young man" in raising the market value 300 per cent.

With the spring of 1835, came a flood of immigration beyond the dreams of all, save possibly John Stephen Wright. By June 150 new buildings had gone up. Land salesmen swarmed and the speculative fever drove even the placid and generally indifferent old French traders into the mood of the Yankee invaders. As 1834 ended, Chicago could count 1,800 citizens where only 350, by the most optimistic view, had lived a year before.

Deacon Wright, for all that he had established his family in a new home at the southwest corner of Michigan and Madison, and was giving some time to his store, found himself already in the shadow of his 19-year-old son. The boy ran the "Prairie Store" and yet had plenty of time for real estate projects. Across the counter, on the streets, in the taverns he preached the future of Chicago.

Before the fire of such belief, Deacon Wright could do little more than cautiously consent when on October 15, the boy bought some forty-four acres south of 12th Street, between State and the lake, paying some $35,000. Twenty-two months later he was offered $50,000 for less than half of it, and some 20 years later saw its value estimated at $1,750,000 without improvements.

Through the winter, speculation kept throbbing in Chicago even though ice stopped lake traffic. The boy knowing that, in the matter of immigration, it was merely the pause before the storm, bought forty acres close to the town's boundary on January 27 of the new year 1835. On May 28, the Federal Government was to open a land office in Chicago, and hold the first acreage sale in this part of the nation. A great rush and boom would result. On May 11 young John bought two lots for $5,200 and saw them in eighteen months climb to a value of $25,000. On that same May 11 he bought 80 acres for $6,000 and saw them 25 years later valued at $1,500,000. And on May 13 he gave $1,300 for forty acres on the outskirts of Chicago—acres which within 20 years were priced at $200,000.

By the middle of May of that year, 1835, the torrent of speculators had crashed down upon the town. Every inn and tavern was jammed with guests, three in a bed and all over the floor. Residents took in roomers and boarders to the point of suffocation. Immigrants slept in or beside their wagons on the streets, while on the outskirts of the town, circling on the prairie like a gigantic barricade against Indians, stood white prairie schooners with their horses and oxen tethered on the grassy expanse beyond.

A "land mania" of huge proportions was gripping the West and this sale of Indian lands in Chicago sent it spiraling upward. Paper money, issued under varying State laws, flooded the whole country and gave impetus to the speculation.

William B. Ogden, a New Yorker who had come out to examine family investments already made in Chicago, attended the Government auction sales and gasped to see crazy people pay such prices for these wild, wet lands.

Professional speculators, hearing how, at Chicago, fortunes were being made in a day, fell upon wide sweeps of the prairie, laying out towns, cities and offering lots for sale. Maps embossed in glaring colors and picturing public squares, churches, schools were thrust under the noses of excited buyers. It was later said that on these gaudy prospectuses all known rivers and creeks were lined with towns and covered with busy canal boats, and that fictitious streams were adorned with grandiose dams and wharves. An onlooker wrote, "Not the puniest brook on the shore of the lake (Michigan) was suffered to remain without a city at its mouth."

Who was to doubt the future of such arteries when, within a year, so shallow and dull a stream as Garlic Creek could become the famous Chicago River with warehouses along its banks and a harbor being dug at its outlet?

Following the example of the Government, private companies held land auctions, fanning the hysteria till "the prairies of Illinois, the forests of Wisconsin, and the sand hills of Michigan presented a chain almost unbroken, of suppositious villages and cities."

Young Wright, riding the wave, balanced his books on his twentieth birthday July 15, 1835, and found that he had $1,225 in the bank, debts of $9,511.29 and real estate worth some $90,000. He was as much a prodigy at business as at Greek.

Around him, Chicago grew more turbulent. Drinking had passed far beyond the genial carousing in Mark Beaubien's tavern. Gambling had grown from sleepy card games between Indians and half-breeds in the sun to "gaming hells" and professional card games. Where tipsy Indians had only months before provided excitement by brandishing tomahawks at each other, now flashy gambling men from the Southern rivers and the New York tenderloins shot it out with derringers.

On August 18 of that strident year of 1835, the Indians, thousands of them, came to town for their formal farewell to their hereditary lands. When the final papers were signed, the bucks stripped to their breech-clouts, doused their skins with war paint, adorned their hair with feathers, and did their "Dance of Blood" through the streets. Braves bending, shrieking, stamping, waving weapons, to the throb of their drums, they promenaded the town, executing their convulsions before each log cabin. As their frenzy mounted, with eyes rolling, mouths foaming, tongues screeching, hatchets splitting sod, white women, watching from cabin windows, hid their eyes and some fainted. An Eastern immigrant, John D. Caton, thought it was like seeing a picture of hell, itself, and a carnival of condemned spirits.

Huldah Dewey Wright, for all that she was fresh from the white-washed serenity of a New England college town, could stand the privations of this raw, red frontier. But her schoolteacher past dominated her and always she kept thinking that something had to be done for the illiterate children who played around the feet of the gamblers and the Indians. Miss Chappel's school was struggling along as best it could in the old log cabin which young Wright had first rented from Mark Beaubien, but it was already outgrown, hopelessly inadequate.

John Stephen Wright later said that it was this passion of his mother's that had impelled him to build, in 1835, a school building for Chicago—the first in the city's history. "The honor is due to my sainted mother. . . . Interested in an infant school, she wanted the building and it was built." Wright paid Joseph Meeker, the carpenter, $505.93 for it, the structure rising on part of the First Presbyterian Church lot on Clark Street.

There was to remain in some people's minds the belief that Wright had been too modest in his story of why the school was built. The Reverend Jeremiah Porter, who was in a position to know, said, in after years, that "John S. Wright was so much interested in Miss Chappel's school that he built a schoolhouse for it at his own expense."

Other observers, familiar with John Stephen Wright's attitude toward family matters, as illustrated by his extreme affection for his own children, wondered if he did not pay excessive honor to his father and mother and deprecate his own acts when, in later life, he came to recall early days in Chicago.

The fact remained that if his mother did inspire him to the historic action, it was to her son and not to her husband that she turned. The boy was worth some $90,000 at the time and could well afford it. That same year he presented his mother with 320 acres of land that he had acquired near the Kankakee River, worth, he estimated, more than $3,000.

With not only the town, but his mother, recognizing his capacity and responsibility, the young man at twenty wanted to escape his father's store and give all his time to the business in which he had already made a sizeable fortune. His brother Timothy was ready to take his place in the "Prairie Store," so John Stephen in December, 1835, persuaded his father to accept a lot worth $2,000 and declare him free. Legally bound to his father's service until he was twenty-one, John Stephen thus secured formal release seven months in advance of schedule.

He was one of the most prominent citizens of the rising young city when, in February, he went to New York with his father, who was buying a new stock of merchandise. But he met swift deflation in the Brooklyn home of his Uncle Amasa. When he had bought land for this uncle he had made it clear, he thought, that he was working as a partner; now, however, he discovered that the older man had been using him merely as an errand boy. Uncle Amasa blandly pocketed the profits from the deals John Stephen had made for him, and gave the boy $100—a mere tip. And, according to John Stephen's later statements, Amasa was, moreover, still nominally in debt to him on Chicago deals pending at the time.

John Stephen Wright never forgot this treatment, particularly as he found other Eastern business men, by contrast, accepting him as an equal. The forty acres, which he had bought the previous year, he sold in New York on April 10, 1836, for $10,000 and, finding the market lively, sold other Chicago lots for $50,000 more, receiving two-thirds of the money in cash.

Back home in the spring of 1836, he bought new lands, keying his purchases to the eternal picture, in his imagination, of the city's stupendous future. By the end of '36 his

holdings included 7,000 acres, and the value of this, added
to that of his lots, made him worth more than $200,000, all
of which, as he afterwards wrote, he had acquired "without any assistance, even from my father, never having
used his money for my operations, the store being his and
for conducting it, only my expenses having been paid."

Deacon Wright, alarmed at his son's whirlwind success
and never having understood his imaginativeness anyway,
began pressing the boy to settle down into some well-
established business. Still a Puritan, tuned more to the
prim mental habits of New England than to the flam-
boyant recklessness of the West, he feared lest his son become nothing but a speculator in land.

John Stephen described it: "At that age (twenty-one)
it seemed desirable in every way to have regular occupation to promote good habits, and in accordance with my
father's wishes, I purchased in 1836 a warehouse and
dock-lots, to engage in the shipping business, which cost
$23,500." This only brought his total indebtedness up to
$25,000, and with $20,000 due him on his land deals, and his
highly valuable lots and acreage apparently well secured,
the goose hung high.

That the shipping venture was against his better judgment was quite likely. So close a friend of the family as
the Reverend Porter said that when John Stephen was
worth $200,000, "he proposed resting from money making,
and travel in Europe, but was persuaded to remain at
home." Having agreed to the step, John Stephen entered
into a contract to sell twenty of his acres for $50,000 so
that he would have ample cash on hand for any emergency.
His father urged him not to do it, as there was no immediate need.

Throughout the fall and winter word came that money
was tightening in the East and that hard times were
coming. The West began to feel the contraction of credit,

but Wright, always bursting with optimism, brushed such tremors aside. It was incredible to him that sensible men should doubt the future of Chicago investments. The city's situation was the same; the rich, black prairies, rapidly filling with settlers, were still there. What of real value had changed?

Oblivious to all warnings, he opened his warehouse and docks in May, 1837, hung his sign, "John S. Wright; Storage, Forwarding and Commission," over the door of his office on Water Street, and faced the future with enthusiasm.

But the tide did not turn. The panic struck the West with shattering force. Money disappeared. Business in the city—Chicago had obtained a city charter in March, 1837—was soon conducted with tickets reading, "Good for ten cents at our store" or "Good for one shave." Small boys managed to drop a great many "Good for one drink" pasteboards into a collection box at church one Sunday. The bubble of Chicago real estate burst, and the price of lots fell back to the level of 1834, and in some cases to that of '33. A contemporary report said, "The land resounded with the groans of ruined men and the sobs of defrauded women." The detonation of crashing banks was in the air, old line commercial houses collapsed.

Before the panic had begun, and due, as he said, "to the merest accident," young Wright's $50,000 sale of land had failed to go through, and as his debtors began to fail him, the lack of this large sum began to pinch. Instead of being secure, he felt the tide of disaster rising to engulf him, too. To hold onto the warehouse and docks he had to sacrifice one piece of property after another. To get $6,000 he had to surrender acreage worth $100,000 a few months before. One property worth $12,000 went for $900, and so on, down, down, down! His Uncle Amasa, whom he had enriched without reward, refused to come to his aid.

Each day he thought the storm had spent its fury and the sun of public confidence would break through the clouds. Fear and hysteria must wear themselves out. Even when he was nearing the end of his solvency, he was optimistic enough to place an advertisement for his commission business in the opening issue of the first Chicago newspaper, the *Democrat*. The date was April 9, 1839.

But by 1840 he was stripped of all his land and his commission business. It had been the latter that had sunk him. What had ruined him was not his buoyant Western faith in Chicago real estate, but his father's thrifty, New England Puritan insistence upon his acquiring a safe, conservative business. Dutiful son that he was, he made no recriminations against the Deacon, saying only in later years, "It was not so much speculation in real estate as engaging in mercantile business that involved me."

Deacon Wright in September, 1836, had expanded his business, establishing a branch store at Pekatonica, later called Rockton, on Rock River, some eighty miles northwest of Chicago, with his son Timothy and a New England immigrant of attractive piety, J. Ambrose Wight, in charge.

With his father thriving even during the panic, John Stephen might have returned in some fashion to the store, but he chose differently. It was too late in his development to become the preacher his mother had always wanted him to be, but he could give himself to public causes and travel the prairies as if he were, indeed, a circuit rider.

CHAPTER IV

"The Old Doctor"

DURING the three years in which he had handled grain and merchandise on commission, Wright had penetrated far into the prairies by horseback, buggy or stagecoach in those sections where stage lines were maintained. He had pushed his saddle-horse along Indian trails where prairie grass stood higher than his head, he had trotted over immense meadows of shorter grass where flowers of all colors waved in the wind, and through groves —those infrequent islands of trees in the grassy sea— where wild fruit hung—cherries, plums, grapes, paw-paws.

He passed acres of briars where blackberries dripped, acres of grass where the juice of wild strawberries stained his horse red to the knees. He stopped at log cabins so crudely made that, as the saying went, "a woman could throw a cat out between the logs in any direction."

A rapid and engaging conversationalist, brilliant and flashing with ideas, Wright was a welcome visitor in the lonely cabins, and, years later, he would glow when he talked about the scope of his acquaintance among the prairie farmers.

When he rode to the northwest, to the Rock River, he would talk with J. Ambrose Wight, and hear that Vermont immigrant deplore the lack of religion and education on the frontier. Later on Wright got his friend to describe on paper the Rock River country as it had been in 1836-37, and Ambrose Wight told how there had been no stagecoach roads and how pork at $30 and flour at $20 a barrel had been hauled with extreme difficulty. "Nobody owned the land. We were all 'squatters' in Congressional parlance. ... The whole community got called out about once a fortnight, more or less, to adjust some dispute between a settler and an interloper. This they did sometimes by simple arbitration, sometimes by tearing down the cabin of the claim jumper about his ears. . . . Indians and blackbirds were very plentiful, and women very scarce. The Indians did very little harm, but the blackbirds destroyed the first crops of about everything. The cornfields had to be guarded by men, dogs and muskets; with poor success at that. It was one of the prophecies of those times, among certain vegetable philosophers, that this region would certainly never be available for farming purposes on account of those birds."

Coons, crows, prairie chickens, wild geese, and, in places, wild swans rivaled the blackbirds in destructiveness. Flies and mosquitoes, breeding in the long grass and in the swamps which dotted the prairie, were blood-thirsty. One farmer described them as "so bad that cows would crawl into the smoke and stand all but in the very fire kindled by settlers to keep them away. Poor horses ran races nightly to be rid of them."

When Wright's travels took him north of Chicago, up near the borderline of Cook and Lake counties, he might see, anywhere within a dozen miles radius of the village Rand, a sight that was familiar to the settlers—a brown pony pacing the trails with something that, at a distance, might be either a man or a monkey in the saddle. Sometimes the strange creature would be carrying a tree whose top and branches hid it altogether—a tree on horseback.

This was the famous "Old Doctor," or, as he was sometimes called, "The Old Sucker," Dr. John A. Kennicott, whose passion for bettering the lives of the settlers was to make him, in time, one of the most influential men in Illinois. A pioneer in prairie horticulture, the first great nurseryman in northern Illinois, father of the still more famous Major Robert Kennicott, naturalist and explorer, "The Old Sucker" doctored men's soil and dooryards as well as their bodies. Nor did he stop with that; he labored with the pen, oratory and persuasion for some of the most revolutionary steps in public education.

Twelve years older than Wright, "The Old Doctor" had a more cosmopolitan background and a greater wealth of scientific lore than the younger man had heretofore met in the West. Born not far from Saratoga, New York, in 1802, the second of fourteen children, Kennicott had, as he later recalled, "had charge of his father's Merino sheep, orchard, garden and nursery before the War of 1812," displaying thereby a precocity that put him in Wright's own class.

His father's face "was ever set toward the West," and by the time the family settled in Western New York State in 1817 or '18, the boy was, as he liked to say in later years, "the best ax-man and general wood-ranger of any boy of my age and size." Heavy shouldered and stooping, he had been singularly small in body and limbs, looking even in maturity like a trim schoolboy from the shoulders down, and never standing more than five feet, five inches high.

"But I was," said he, in describing his youth, "miserably ignorant of all matter taught in schools." Avidly he read everything he could lay his hands upon, and once made his way to a common school in Chautauqua county where he managed to stay thirty days, feasting feverishly. Forced to hurry home at the end of that time, he immediately set about passing on to his younger brothers and sisters what he had learned, and he soon expanded, starting a common country school of his own.

Forever asking questions and burning with vitality and endurance, he was teaching school in Buffalo by 1828, and

"The Old Doctor,"
Dr. John A. Kennicott

Hiram Kennicott

"The Grove," home of Dr. John A. Kennicott

at the same time clerking in an apothecary's shop, studying medicine and sending poems to newspapers in Albany, Philadelphia and Buffalo. Later that year he got a degree in medicine from the college at Fairfield, New York, and was off on a tour of exploration, hunting for a location that would interest him. Practising medicine, lecturing on science and horticulture, and writing poems and articles for newspapers, he journeyed through Canada, Detroit, Cincinnati, Louisville, Natchez, Jackson and New Orleans, arriving in the latter metropolis in the winter of 1828-29.

His insatiable energy soon established him as principal of a school and founder of the *Louisiana Recorder*, which he later described as "the first literary, scientific and religious paper ever printed in New Orleans." To fatten the literary quality of the sheet, he imported his brother James from home, and saw James become an author and playwright of local fame. Hurrying back to Buffalo in 1830, he married Mary Shutts Ransom and brought her to New Orleans, where they lived until 1836, when roseate letters from a brother in northern Illinois, coupled with the outbreak of fever in New Orleans, prompted him to resign his post as superintendent of the Male Orphan Asylum and move north.

Prior to 1834 one of his brothers, Levi, had moved to Chicago, but had quickly waded out of the town to higher land in Lake county some twenty miles north of the swamp village, and had sent for his family to come to the Promised Land. A brother Hiram, destined to be John S. Wright's close friend, had come on in 1834, settling near the crossroads settlement of Half Day on the Aux Plaines (later Desplaines) River. The family energy was in Hiram, too, and he became not only the first justice of the peace in Lake county, but the builder of its first store, first sawmill, first gristmill.

To join him came his father, mother and younger

brothers and sisters from New York, while up from New Orleans came Dr. John A., with a wife and two infants. Soon there was a great concentration of Kennicotts in the neighborhood, what with Hiram owning 960 acres where Arlington was later to rise, Dr. John A. owning 250 acres some four miles away, William, another brother, owning 360 nearby, Brother Alonzo 80 more, and the father and mother with two unmarried daughters, on 78 close at hand. William and another brother, Jonathan, were soon studying medicine under Dr. John A., and in time went to Chicago to take rank among the leading dentists of the city.

Destined to become more famous than all the Kennicotts was Robert, who was a baby of one year when his father, "The Old Doctor," started establishing the farm and orchard which, known as "The Grove," was to become famous for its view, its rare and beautiful flowers and its sweeps of fruit trees and berry bushes. Humble though the farmhouse was, it was celebrated for its hospitality. A drive out to the Grove was in the 1840's and '50's "the" thing to do of a Sunday afternoon in the "refined" social circles of Chicago.

The baby, Robert, second of Dr. John's seven children (Hiram across the field was to have twelve) was sickly and the father, contriving to keep him outdoors as he grew up, interested him in natural history so effectively that the boy, while scarcely out of infancy, kept a notebook on beetles and bugs he had found in the orchard. By the time he was eighteen, Robert was forwarding specimens of fish to the Smithsonian Institute, at Washington. At twenty he was assisting the naturalist Agassiz, and working on the natural history of Illinois for the Smithsonian. The museums of natural history of the city of Chicago and of Northwestern University were created by him while still in his twenties, and, in 1866, he, a major in the United States Army, was exploring the newly acquired Alaska when death by freezing ended his career.

Closely associated with Dr. John A. though he was, and well aware of his eccentricities and importance, Wright left no such pen portrait of "The Old Doctor" as did one of the sons of Stephen Thacker, a settler of Lake county.

"Not above five feet, five inches in height, slight in build and very stoop shouldered, yet with a physiognomy and an address that would attract attention in any assemblage in the world. . . . His face was thin, long and swarthy . . . a face seamed with deep lines of thought, and eyes that were wonderful . . . forever asking questions, but his eyes always took on a questioning look before the word was spoken . . . that hungry, avaricious mind of his covered a greater variety of subjects than one would think it possible. How many different branches of science his grasping, searching mind covered no one knew. He was an authority among the farmers on almost everything pertaining to farming. It was a common thing when two or three farmers were talking for one of them to remark, 'Well, Dr. Kennicott says so.' . . . He was a thorough and successful farmer . . . he had gotten the best ideas from all the farmers of the surrounding country. . . . His fine memory and vast reading, coupled with the habit of asking questions made him, in time, a kind of moving, talking cyclopedia, diffusing knowledge as he passed along. . . . His mind was constantly rushing from one thing to another, like a bee gathering sweets from every flower. . . . To pass through his orchard with him when he was at leisure was to hear a terse, concise lecture on fruit, the different varieties, the kinds best suited to our climate and soil, and this, too, at a time when the idea was prevalent that Northern Illinois was anything but a fruit country. In his dooryard he had specimens of every variety of shrubbery that he could get hold of. . . . When riding along the road to visit patients, he would sometimes stop his horse and dismount to ex-

amine some strange plant or bush. . . . Whenever he found
a new or rare plant or shrub, he would have some person
living in the vicinity take it up and have it ready for him
on his next trip when he could take it home.

"At his own hearthstone he was simply superb, genial,
friendly, hearty and wholly devoid of all form . . . busy as
a bee in his shirt sleeves, arranging some curious specimen
of plant or shrub or poring over some book of a scientific
character. He was one of the best livers, too . . . and was
a connoisseur in regard to cooking game, which he liked
roasted or broiled at the fireplace. He was a lover of fresh
fish and encouraged the boys to bring them to him whenever they wished to catch them. He always paid fifty or
a hundred per cent more than the boys would ask him. He
would insist upon their taking the cash notwithstanding
he had a book account against the family for medical
services."

Riding a large circuit daily on a brown Canadian mare
pony, whose pacing gait enabled him to sleep in the saddle,
Dr. Kennicott was known to cover sixty miles a day for
six consecutive days in August and September, the season
for chills, fever and ague.

Charging little, supplying medicines free, and treating
the poor and needy with the same courtesy he gave those
who did pay him, he won the affection of the settlers, although there were whispers that he never mentioned religion at all. "The amount he did not collect for professional services must have been large," said the Thacker
boy. "Whatever may have been his religious beliefs, no
physician did more for the poor and suffering. . . .

"He rode in a big saddle, the biggest I think he could
get. It was high behind and before, the pommel coming
high up before him. He would drop the bridle reins over
the horn, rest both hands upon the pommel, lean forward
and rest his weight upon them. He had a way of huddling

himself down in the saddle and humping up his back, which gave him a most ludicrous appearance. At a distance it was hard to determine whether it was a man or monkey in the saddle."

In 1849, "The Old Doctor," looking back on the days when both he and John S. Wright had ridden the prairies, set the years 1840 and 1841 as "the era from which we date the commencement of fruit culture in Northern Illinois though for some years thereafter we were all poor, having been drained by our land purchases and more especially by the 50 per cent per annum which we had to pay those who kindly loaned us a good share of money.

"Few cared about planting trees until we could be tolerably certain we were planting upon our own land and of this we had no evidence until after the surveys and no security until after the land sales. The last of these events occurred only about eight years ago and the former the year before."[1]

Traveling widely over the state in 1835 and '36, he "did not see a fruit tree or even as much as a currant bush this side of Springfield, though I was told there were some seedling trees near Peoria and afterwards I saw apple trees near the garrison ground in Chicago, planted by General Beaubien while Chicago was a remote trading post. The first occupants were of the true squatter breed, ... so that no attention was paid to orcharding."

With the growth of Chicago in the late 1830's and early '40's, he saw the growth of "Hoosier trees." Volunteer sprouts from the pits of fruit sold by peddlers who came up from the banks of the Wabash, grew readily in Chicago soil, but were worthless and it was not until 1844 and '45 that cultivated trees were seen in dooryards.

Since the hard times had settled upon the West, the rate of Illinois' yearly increase in population had been cut

(1) Kennicott report of North American Pomological Convention for Illinois, in Report of U. S. Commissioners of Patents, 1849, Part II.

in half, and some men estimated that more people were
leaving the state than entering it. The population in 1838-
39 might have been around 450,000, but that was not what
it should have been, considering the vast quantities of
black soil available at $1.25 an acre. Nor was it convincing
to serious thinkers like Wright and Kennicott that the
money panic was responsible for the decline in immigration. With jobs gone and Easterners foreclosing mort-
gages, there should have been plenty of men to leap at the
chance to start anew on the cheap, fertile lands of the
West. Famines and depressions in Europe would be
enough to send the landless clear across the Atlantic and
on by boat and wagon to these same open acres.

To the group of New Englanders with whom Wright
became intimate on the prairies, it was apparent that what
was hampering settlement was the general ignorance of
how to live and how to produce on the strange prairie
ground. Always before in the westward push of American
immigration, the forest had been both obstacle and friend
to man. Although the settler had to toil prodigiously to
clear it away, it had given him cheap material for house,
barn, fences and fuel. But on the treeless bosom of the
prairie this traditional pattern was useless.

Such islands of timber as did arise above the grassy
sea had been included in the claims of the first squatters,
the usual thing being for a man to take one-third of his
acreage in timber and two-thirds open range.

Unable to buy timber land either because it was occupied or because speculators had bought it up and were
holding it for a fabulous future price, thousands of immigrants had shrunk from trying to take up claims on the
great bare bosom of the prairie. There was no stone for
houses or fences. Even if logs and rails could be bought,
the mud was too deep for hauling save in a few months
of the year. So much of the land was in swamps or marsh-

es that malaria and the ague were regarded as inescapable. Milk sickness, also called the "puking complaint," was a deadly visitor.

Another awesome barrier to the eager settler was the task of breaking the prairie. Grasses regarded as peculiar to the region covered the prairie and to the depth of twelve or fifteen inches sent down roots as large as a man's finger, forming a sward so tough as to defy the cast iron plow which settlers brought with them from the East. By hitching eight to sixteen oxen to a plow, and halting often to sharpen the dulling ploughshare with a file, the settler could turn the sod, but it was a slow and expensive business, dismaying enough to turn many settlers back to Indiana or divert them to Missouri, or, indeed, cause them to retreat clear to the East, whence they had come.

John D. Caton, the lawyer and farmer of Ottawa, Illinois, with whom young Wright discussed prairie farming, said that when he had arrived from New York State in 1833 he discovered that whatever he had learned of farming back East had to be learned over again here. Other influential men told Wright that "nothing in the practice of our Eastern neighbors is practical when applied to our prairies."

Wright discovered among certain of his fellow "Yankee" emigrants a frank facing of the problem: they must reform the public's idea of agriculture if the prairie was ever to become the paradise they had imagined. Reform was a word that came easily to New Englanders. Theirs was the duty to convert others to the truth as it had been bred in them across generations of churchgoing. Now, in the 1830s, the Yankees were out to achieve reform in the paths of temperance, women's rights, and slavery.

Here on the prairies they saw that whatever ideas of agriculture had been adopted were mainly those of the Southern or Border States, thanks to the earlier settlement of the lower portion of Illinois' area by immigrants from Kentucky, Tennessee and Virginia. Scrub cattle, razor-back hogs and thin horses, better for saddles than for harness, were the usual livestock. Rotation of crops, the sheltering of stock, scientific farming, as a general thing, were ignored.

That the characteristically Southern style of farming should have been accepted as far north as the gates of Chicago, was noted by one of the prairie pioneers who influenced John S. Wright in 1840. He was Dr. John Thomas who had practiced medicine and farming 40 miles from Richmond, Virginia, before migrating to Long Grove, in LaSalle county, Illinois. Seeking, as he wrote to Wright, to better himself, he had "determined to sell out of the Virginia system, in which everything degenerates— land, cattle, hogs, wheat, etc. and in the fertile West begin again. . . . Virginia has been impoverished to such an extent by the starved system of agriculture which consists in hard cropping, close grazing, and non-manuring (except for the tobacco patch) that it has become . . . reduced to such sterility that considerable stock is imported from Kentucky." He asked "How in the name of reason, can farmers get milk from cattle starved for want of food and comfortable shelter? In Virginia they get no hay, no beets nor other roots; nothing in fact but a few shucks, a small portion of damaged straw, and the scanty pickings called 'boots' which remain on the corn stalks after the fodder is pulled.

"And I perceive, even in this rich country, things are reduced almost if not quite, to the same level."

The first settlers in the 1830s had, in the main, thought of life on "the wild prairies" as an adaption of the Southern plantation system so far as size of farm was concerned, and as an imitation of the dawning range system of the Southwest, so far as occupation went. With land so cheap and grass so plentiful the easy road to riches had seemed to lie in the direction of a large claim of "Congress land" filled with herds of cattle which grazed on the open range, and with just enough land tilled to supply food for human beings. It was thought that enough prairie grass could be cut to keep cattle through the freezing months, and that pigs, cows and horses could winter in the lee of haystacks.

Striking first for the timbered land, these early settlers had it well monopolized by 1841 and had already begun to think of themselves as the vested interests, the early risers, the pioneers who were entitled to the fruits of their conquest. For all the primitive nature of their lives, theirs was essentially the aristocratic system, the baronial plan in embryo, each man looking toward the day when he would be a cattle baron, letting his herds roam, free as grass and air, upon the public domain, and keeping up his guard against immigrants who proposed cutting up this open grazing land with fence and plow.

Late in the summer the cattle baron, his sons and neighbors from far-off gathered their cattle in, and sold the steers to drovers who, starting from Missouri, swept across the prairies of Iowa and Illinois and on across Indiana to Madison, Fayette and Union counties in Ohio, where feeders, buying with funds advanced by the banks of that region, assembled the lean, grass-fed steers, "fatted" them on corn and then drove them by easy stages to the markets of the Atlantic seaboard.

Torrents of wild Missouri steers, their long horns tossing as they raced ahead of horsemen, many of whom were "Mexican rangers," crossed Illinois, their numbers sometimes reaching 2,000 to the trail-herd.

Here and there across the prairie had risen cattle barons like the Funk Brothers, Isaac and Jesse, and "the Napoleon of cattle," Jacob Strawn, men who owned from 16,000 to 30,000 acres of land and controlled thousands more of open range acres, and who sent to markets herds of from 1,000 to 1,600 steers.

It so happened that the Funks and Strawn were public-spirited but the cattlemen as a class were reactionary, holding to the faith that the destiny of the prairie was that of a thinly-settled cow-country. They had made the laws, and like true conservatives, thoroughly entrenched, would fight for them. It was a grazier's, not a grain-grower's, law which decreed that the property owner must fence in his crops and protect them against the wandering herds. And the cattleman asked, "Supposing the law were to be reversed and the grazier forced to fence in his herds while the prairie grain-grower was permitted to plant and reap without the expense of buying rails, where would the rails come from?"

The cattleman pointed out the high cost of any kind of fence strong enough to turn the half-wild hogs which settlers kept for winter butchering. He maintained that only the long-legged rapacious Southern hog was suited to the country, since it foraged for itself and produced the lean, hard, red meat, which when smoked in the leisurely and artistic fashion of the South, produced the only American bacon and ham that England would buy. On the smaller farms of New England, larger, softer, fatter hogs were being raised, but the general taste was for the lean meat. The difference between the Northern and Southern hogs—as well as between the civilizations of the two sections—was humorously described in the *Farmer's Library and Monthly Journal of Agriculture*, by its editor, John Stuart Skinner, who had commenced agricultural journalism in the United States with the publication of the *American Farmer* at Baltimore in 1819.

Said Skinner: "The hog leads, in the North and in the South, a very different sort of life, reversing, as some would say, the habits of their owners, respectively.

"Here in New England the function and habits of the grunter consist entirely in eating and sleeping. Stuffed to obesity, his faculties uncultivated and dormant while his carcass turns all into fat.

"Wild Hog—He came here from the south somewhere," an illustration from *The Prairie Farmer*, April, 1852—part of its campaign of ridicule against the razor back and prairie pikes.

"How different the destiny and habits of his brethren in the South. There, notwithstanding the heat of the climate, he leads a life of labor and vigilance." Where the Northern hog was confined, "shut out from the light of heaven and exempt from the animating excitement of an empty stomach," the hog in the South "traverses the fields and woods and meadows and mountains from the rising of the sun to the going down thereof in search of creature comforts, as persimmons and acorns and nuts, in company with rivals, brothers, sisters and cousins with all of whom he sleeps o' nights without sense or deed of sin or shame.

"Sometimes you will see them all waiting for the fruit by its sound as it falls, like boys 'round a bandy-ball. Kept thus constantly on the trot, working hard though at times roguishly for their living, the Southern hog has time to grow and acquire the name of hog before he dies, weighing not more than 160 at 18 months, if it can be helped. Thus his flesh acquires a proper texture and consistency of hardness, as it is termed, which, if cured by a good, thrifty-managing, well-bred and brought-up housewife, comes out of the smoke-house worth, as bacon, its weight in gold—red, juicy, savory and tender, and yet firm, neither too salty or too fresh, too hard or too soft."

On the prairie these pigs were savage roamers, eating baby fawns when they could seize them, as readily as they did acorns, roots, crawfish, snakes, anything, everything. Huge of head and weak of shank, they were nicknamed "land sharks," "land pikes," "alligators," "prairie pointers," "prairie racers," "prairie breakers," or "squealing devils."

In towns and villages they adapted themselves to metropolitan life with great good nature, appropriating the contents of swill barrels, if necessary, but preferring to consume garbage lying in the streets where the average townswife obligingly threw it. When Chicago progressed to the point of having board sidewalks, in the 1840s, the hogs approved, and slept blissfully thereon, as if to shame those who derided them as wild and dirty by nature.

The shame of raising pigs by the Southern method on the prairie was described by a newcomer from New England, a settler at Burnt Prairie, Wayne county, Illinois, in a letter to *The Maine Farmer* which was "published pretty close under the edge of the sunrise."

"Hogs," he said, "find nuts, roots, etc., frequently remaining out all winter without being fed at all. They are generally let alone till near two years old and then taken up to fatten for six weeks and killed at Christmas. The hogs are hunted out of the woods and bottom, a dozen or more put into a rail pen without floor or covering, and corn in the shuck thrown over to them. Of course our falls and winters are generally rainy, and the hog pens muddy; and if the hog wishes to have a clean coat, he has only to stand up during the first shower. The length of time he will remain clean depends, of course, on his ability or disposition to keep his feet. The water falling into the pen is often all they receive while fattening, many persons never giving a quart of water, pretending that it prevents their fattening. . . . Much of the pork is made in this way. . . . The plain reason for such mismanagement is an aversion to labor. I know land turned out as worn out and new land cleared to take its place, where I do not think the plow ever ran three inches deep and where the manure is in the old stables eighteen or twenty years of age. In this way of mismanagement the settler 'comes out even,' makes 'what will do him,' and lives to suit his fancy on the labor of about four months a year. This gives him the 'hog and hominy' so often quoted as Western fare, and on it he is content to live. Now what a curious Yankee could fix out of this hog and hominy! . . . Well, we will begin with the little roaster and follow with a bit of fresh shoat and roast pork. Then we have at killing time the head and feet, bones, ribs and harslet, accompanied with a few sausages. Then comes ham, shoulder, middling and jowl, pickled pork and lard. With this dry grub we have pone, dodger, johnny cake and hoe cake, a little hulled corn, samp and hominy, hasty pudding, baked corn pudding, roasting ear, boiled corn, fried corn, popped corn, suet cake and a sip of water gruel."

Selling the extra "prairie racers" to the "pork-barrellers" along the Illinois, Ohio and Mississippi Rivers, the early settlers were content with low profits, if, indeed, there was any profit at all in driving the beasts to market by leisurely stages. Sometimes farmers, clubbing together, would drive as many as 1,000 hogs from Southern Illinois to Cincinnati, drifting along at from 6 to 10 miles a day.

To reform these farm methods required a great deal more than to provide faster transportation to market.

Farmers must be taught to raise heavier-bodied animals
and fatten them in confinement on their own farms instead of selling them, half-fat, to professional drovers, as
they usually did. They must be convinced that it was
better to plough up the prairie grass, even if it were free
on the open range, and to substitute for it enclosed fields
of clover and timothy. Prairie grass died in August, and
was far less nutritious as hay than the cultivated grasses.
Heavy breeds of cattle, blooded stock, must be brought on
and reared in place of the lean, scrubby steers. Draft horses
and mules must replace the slow oxen as work animals.

With some of the advocates of these reforms, profit
was the motive; they saw that the change would mean
wealth to the community and themselves. With others,
such as Wright and Kennicott, the primary motive was
pity for the children who grew up in lonely cabins, with
scarcely more culture than Indians, marooned in the groves
almost as completely as Marquesans on an island, so far
as schooling was concerned—victims of the thinly scattered nature of population.

Even counting the influx of educated Easterners in the
northern part of the state, one in every 18 citizens could
neither read nor write, and illiteracy among children was
appalling. From what he had seen, Wright concluded "that
four-fifths of the teachers of common schools would not
pass an examination in the rudiments of English education and most of them have taken to teaching because they
hadn't anything in particular to do."

Another authority described the better schools of the
prairies as forced to depend upon the community preacher
or doctor giving instruction as a side-line, while the average school had to rely upon "an ignorant man who had
picked up a little 'book larnin' which he was willing to
impart to the children in exchange for the parents' wheat,
pork, hogs, beeswax, tallow, deerskins, wool and young

cattle. Too often he was a shiftless, drunken straggler who still retained some part of his early requirements."[2]

Admittedly the schools on the frontier were far below those of the older states back East, and yet the State Superintendent of Schools for New York was denouncing his own commonwealth's system, and issuing a formal report that specifically exposed "the nakedness and deformity of the great majority of the schools, the comfortless and dilapidated buildings, absent panes, stilted benches, yawning roofs and muddy, mouldering floors ... and many of the self-styled teachers who lash and dogmatize in these miserable tenements of humanity, are shown to be too low, vulgar, obscene, intemperate, and utterly incompetent to teach anything good. Thousands of the young are repelled ... and contract a durable horror for books by ignorant, injudicious and even cruel modes of instruction. . . . And it is in these miserable abodes of filth and dirt, deprived of wholesome air or exposed to the assaults of the elements, with no facilities for exercise or relaxation, with no conveniences for prosecuting their studies ... and driven by dire necessity to violate the most common rules of decency and modesty. . . . Here the instinctive delicacy of the young female, the characteristic ornament of her sex, is to be expanded into maturity by precept and example."

At home, Wright heard his mother lamenting the deplorable character of the teaching her younger children were receiving as compared with that which her three older boys, John Stephen, Timothy and Walter, had been given in New England. Since coming to the frontier, she had seen her young boys and girls, Anne Eliza, Edward, and Frances Sarah pass into adolescence without receiving anything of the advantages which the excellent schools, Williams College, and her brother,

(2) Historical sketches of the State Normal and the Universities of Illinois, by W. L. Pillsbury, 17th Biennial Report, Supt. of Public Instruction, July 1, 1866-June 30, 1888.

the famous Professor Dewey, had given the older boys.

It was not enough that her son John Stephen should have built an infant school for Chicago. He must do more, and the fact that his wealth was seeping away, merely meant, both to him and to her, apparently, that he would have more time to labor for the thing she loved best— education. He had given some time in 1838 as secretary of the Chicago Colonization Society, for the city's population was standing still in the season of hard times and energy was needed to revive faith in a destiny as manifest as Chicago's. With the taste of public service and civic promotion in his mouth, he turned his mind toward an organization which promised him the shortest cut toward betterment of the schools—the formation of progressive farmers into a society.

In 1838, presumably late in the year, a few men with similar ideas met and decided to organize such a body. In January, 1839, a delegation, with John S. Wright as chief spokesman, journeyed to Vandalia, the State Capital, to ask the Legislature to charter the Union Agricultural Society, "for the sole purpose of instruction and science, and improvements in scientific and practical agriculture and the mechanical arts in the counties of LaSalle, Will, Cook, McHenry and Kane." On February 19 the act of incorporation was passed, with Wright as one of fifty trustees, and also one of the ten commissioners empowered to sell $10,000 of stock in the non-profit corporation.

At twenty-three years of age, the Wright boy was bidding farewell to the career of a moneyed man and was embarking upon the seas of public service.

CHAPTER V

"Little Spark on the Prairie"

FOR all Wright's optimism and enthusiasm, he found the times still too hard for the selling of stock in a philantropic corporation like the Union Agricultural Society. Moreover, it was not until July 8, 1840, that the trustees could be brought together to elect officers. In the courthouse at Juliet (later renamed Joliet) they assembled, chose John S. Wright secretary and Levi Hills of LaSalle county chairman, and then proceeded to ballot on permanent officers. John Dean Caton, soon to be named Chief Justice of the Supreme Court of Illinois, was made president. Wright was elected corresponding and recording secretary. William B. Ogden, the financier of Chicago who within a little more than a decade was to be known as "The Railroad King of the West," was chosen treasurer.

Six, and probably all eight, of the officers had come from New England or New York State. Of the fifty original trustees, twenty-eight could be proved, a century later, to have come from those Yankee regions. Of the remaining twenty-two trustees, three were from Ohio, one from Pennsylvania, and although the remaining eighteen came from unrecorded States, the majority of them lived in communities peopled almost wholly by Yankee emigrants.

But the new authority did not lessen Wright's difficulties in enrolling members for the society, since his campaign ran head-on into another—one that had the nation agog—"The Log Cabin Campaign" of William Henry Harrison for the presidency of the United States.

The Whigs, blaming the long dominant Democrats for the prolonged hard times, had resurrected the old Indian fighter, Harrison, from his farm in Ohio, and orating wildly about his virtues as a frontiersman, farmer and Indian fighter, were attempting to beguile the voters, and the Western farmers in particular, away from their allegiance to the Democracy of Andrew Jackson. The Whigs ridiculed mercilessly the good clothes, cultivated manners and reputedly elegant tastes of the Democratic candidate, President Martin Van Buren. Gigantic rallies with beeves barbecued in frontier style, endless barrels of free whiskey flowing, and miniature log cabins parading on floats, rocked the country.

Unable to make his stock subscription offers heard above the squealing fifes, hammering drums and roaring orators, Wright went to the trustees of the Union Agricultural Society and told them that a newspaper was necessary to the establishment of their society. It should be a periodical that would be as non-political and non-partisan as the established newspapers were biased and prejudiced. He argued that a farm paper could awaken readers to needs which the general papers did not touch.

It was likely that Wright did not stress, in his pleas to the trustees, the purpose that burned deepest inside him—the desire to create a paper that would reform the schools of the State and perhaps of the whole new West. Later he admitted that he had seen how, with the established newspapers indifferent to education, and with a formal school paper necessarily limited in circulation to school teachers themselves, the quickest way to carry his propaganda to the settlers was to interest them in an agricultural paper, which would carry school news as a side line.

Always a compelling salesman, Wright soon led the trustees to appoint a committee, with him as chairman, to investigate the possibilities and report at the next meeting which was to be held at Naperville later in the summer. When the time came Wright announced that the survey showed the thing could be done. Agreeing, the trustees appropriated $100 and asked him to serve as editor, offering him, in lieu of salary "whatever could be made out of 1,000 subscribers," a sum estimated by him to be some $300 a year, if all went well. Above that, the profits were to go toward enlarging the paper.

With what was probably coyness, Wright protested against taking the editorship, saying that he knew nothing of journalism. In reality he never had any hesitation in tackling new projects. While he had never written for newspapers, he had an educational background that made him a marked man on the frontier. He was probably franker later on when he said that he had taken "the editorial charge merely to get the paper started, without the remotest idea of continuing the work for more than a year." At another time he declared he had accepted the post "believing that I could at least make out of it a living till something better offered."

Whatever the shades of his reasonings, it was nevertheless true that he, a youth of 25 who had never worked a day on a farm, became the chief organizer of an agricultural society, and although he had never written a line for publication, became a reporter, editor and publisher of an agricultural monthly.

There were distractions other than the Harrison-Van Buren presidential campaign in that month of September as Wright set himself to his new task. His own bankruptcy had to be adjusted, and then, on September 20, his father died, mourned by the town as "one of the most meritorious pioneers of the city." All churches grieved, for he had done more than work for the Presbyterians. He had helped organize the Chicago Bible Society in 1835, had put his shoulder to the task of assisting the Catholics in October, 1836, to raise the frame of their first church in the city. He had been one of those to sign the call which organized the first school district in 1835 and, in 1837, had joined with other civic-minded citzens in launching Rush Medical College, which was within three years of opening at the time of his death. Living frugally, he left his heirs property which would, in time, be worth $4,000,000. Over half of this amount—$2,500,000—would lie in seventy acres near what was the heart of Chicago—seventy acres left from the original claim his son, John Stephen, with a boy's far-sightedness, had surveyed and preempted for him in 1832, when he, himself, had been far away scouting what he had thought was infinitely more promising territory scores of miles inland.

Though Deacon Wright had left his estate free from danger of the bankruptcy that had struck his eldest son, there was some debt upon it; at least John S. later spoke of "the remnants of my patrimony, which had been saved by borrowing money of my uncle at twenty-five per cent interest, to pay the bank." Values were too low in 1840, and for years thereafter, to allow the heirs to do more than hold onto such of the property as they could.

One effect of the squalor of the political campaign was to convince Wright that the agricultural paper must be kept absolutely free of politics. Never, said he, would it mention the subject, and always it must stick to grass, animals, grain, schools, plants, wind, rain, soil, the things that would be living forces when the names and platforms of politicians were forgotten.

When he was not writing or making arrangements with a job printer in Chicago to print the first edition of 1,300 copies, Wright was darting about the State distributing copies of a prospectus of the paper, pushing other trustees to do the same.

Briskly, almost preemptorily, he managed the society's affairs. On October 5, the jobless and bankrupt youth of 25 wrote to President Caton who, though only three years older, was already a judge, a successful lawyer, farmer and man of affairs, that with time so short he had issued the notice of a trustees' meeting himself, without waiting for the president to do it. "And now I want you to send such a notice of the meeting, and be careful you date it back far enough to give time for it to have reached me, had you sent it previous to the notice being given."

He sternly advised Caton to be on time for the meeting in question, which was to be held in Chicago, October 21. "If you delay your appearance as long as you did at Naperville, it will be dark before we can begin. I meant to have had you explain or apologize to the Society, but forgot it in the hurry. I want you to send me the names of the persons you have appointed on those Committees. I want to publish them in our paper. We shall try hard to have the first number out by the time of our meeting."[1]

In October this first number of *The Union Agriculturalist* appeared, with Wright, as he confessed, awaiting "in fear and trembling" for the public's verdict. He had taken the bull by the horns at the very start, and had made the paper's most controversial article one on schools instead of agriculture. In preparing his copy, he had spent hours under midnight candles digging into statute books and legislative reports, trying to make head or tail out of the chaos into which Illinois' school funds had fallen. Originally the Federal Government had bequeathed to the State a fund for establishing colleges and seminaries, but this had been appropriated by the harassed State Legislature during the panic and was now generally regarded as gone, forever. But Wright made what he later described as "the discovery that the College and Seminary funds had

[1] Wright to Caton, Caton Papers, Library of Congress.

only been *borrowed* by the State, and that in accordance
with the terms of the grants by Congress they could be
used to endow a Normal School or Teachers' seminary."

Wright was agitating many school reforms—the creation of the office of State Superintendent of Schools, and
the extension of legal permission to small localities to tax
themselves to have the kind of schools they desired—but
most important improvement in the caliber of teachers.

How far he was in advance of his time may be judged
from the fact that it had only been in 1836-7 that agitation for teachers' colleges had been begun in New England, and researchers into the educational history of Illinois later concluded that Wright's was "the first definite
proposition for a State Normal School in Illinois."[2]

To launch a new paper with demands for greater public
expenditures staring out from its very first issue, was
perilous in this hour, and Wright was anxious as it came
from the press, but within a few days the whole edition
was gone and the trustees of the Society were urging him
to make the paper a permanent one, to be printed in an
edition large enough to circulate not only in Illinois, but in
Indiana, Wisconsin and Michigan, as well. Flushed with
success, he got out another experimental number in November. In it he proposed that if farm leaders and post-
masters in the West would become subscription agents,
The Union Agriculturalist would appear regularly, commencing formally in January, 1841, in an edition of 2,500
copies, terms $1.00 a year.

The response was encouraging, but Wright, instead of
buckling down to the job of preparing copy, dashed off to
Springfield, the new State capital, to lobby among the
legislators for new school laws. During the month he helped
drum up and manage a convention of educational reformers, and became the secretary of the resultant Illinois

(2) Early Education in Illinois, by W. L. Pillsbury in Biennial Report, Supt. of
Public Instruction, Springfield, Ill., 1886.

State Educational Society which was launched on January 12 of the new year. Throughout December he toiled too, for the formation of the Illinois State Agricultural Society of which he also became secretary when it was definitely organized on January 15. Thoughtfully, he got his paper named as the body's official organ.

His financial failures were now almost forgotten, for here at twenty-five years of age, he was the secretary and virtual manager of three influential societies devoted to public service.

His own soaring optimism had not been able, however, to lobby his school bills through the Legislature. He had signed, and, quite likely written, the memorial which the State Educational Society had pushed upon the solons. He had argued with them day and night, but, as he afterward admitted, "the work was begun at the wrong end." Too few of the lawmakers "cared anything at all about education to have its quality much regarded. Before legislators could be induced to spend money to educate teachers, the people must be made to feel their necessities and cry aloud for improvements."

Wright's memory of these first steps was printed in his paper twelve years after the events, and he evidently had forgotten that among the few legislators who espoused his cause was one representative from Sangamon county, named Abraham Lincoln, who, on December 2, 1840, introduced a resolution "instructing the Committee on Education to inquire about a law to examine the qualifications of persons offering themselves as school teachers." Of many resolutions proposed this was one of the few to remain intact when the Legislature did pass the Common School Act of 1841, an act which, as a whole, was most disappointing to Wright.

Back in Chicago, Wright got out the first formal issue of the paper, making its strongest article a call to the

people to petition their legislators to correct the defects
in the law.

Wright attacked his new problem of editing with the
simplicity of genius and the engaging quality of candor.
He admitted that he was a "numskull" in farm matters,
that he must depend upon his readers, the practical farmers, themselves, to fill its columns with communications.
Since prairie farming was strange, baffling and new, the
settlers must work out their salvation themselves, without
help from Eastern experts, and publish their findings in
The Union Agriculturalist to which he added for the
January issue the subhead *And Western Prairie Farmer*.
The paper must become a forum in which they exchanged
questions, experiences, trials and errors.

"Upon you," he told them, "we must rely for the matter
that is to make this paper interesting and valuable. No
editorial skill can make it what the West demands. . . .
If there should be a word misspelt or a sentence that might
be improved by a little alteration, we will use our en-
deavors to make it right." The personal experiences and
views of uneducated farmers could be of more service to
the West than all the articles of erudite scientists.

The paper was to be a monthly, selling at $1.00 a year,
and since it was not to be operated for profit, but for the
public good, all readers, he declared, should make it their
duty to contribute articles and drum up subscriptions.
"But," he added, "we would rather receive a contribution
than a subscription."

It was the start of a policy soon to be expressed in the
masthead slogan, "Farmers, Write for Your Paper."

Wright appealed to leading farmers of the West to
write for the paper. He needed bell-cows, pump-primers,
if the horny-handed settlers were ever to be led into com-
posing pieces for the paper. Furthermore, the average
farmer commonly scorned "book-farming," and to tempt

him actually to grip a pen and sit up late at night under guttering candles and scratch out informative letters would be a task indeed.

Among the first of the farm leaders to respond to Wright's invitation was Solon Robinson, a remarkable character living just over the State line in Lake county, Indiana, where the Grand Prairie began its westward and southwestward sweep. Robinson had come to the region from Connecticut, via Cincinnati, in 1834. Since 1837 he had been sending interesting descriptions of prairie agriculture to *The Albany* (New York) *Cultivator*, foremost agricultural paper of the East, developing the style that, in time, made him the leading agricultural writer in the country, and famous as the farm editor of Horace Greeley's *New York Tribune*.

Reading the *Cultivator*, while he experimented with the 1840 issues of *The Union Agriculturist*, Wright had written Robinson, asking help. On October 20, 1840, Robinson replied, observing that the hour was ripe for just such a paper as Wright was producing. "Too long," he said, "a false estimation has been put upon farmers, causing farm boys to leave the ways of their fathers' households and go off to the towns and cities to become merchants, mechanics, soldiers, priests, lawyers or loafers. Now, a change is coming over the spirit of the people— agricultural papers are springing up in every State and the spirit will keep on working till the farmer is taught to know and appreciate himself."

Robinson had discovered, of late, that a large mass of his fellow-farmers had "the power to communicate interesting matter to the public, if only they could be roused up." An agricultural paper was the medium for rousing them.

He foresaw Wright's paper as "the little spark, scarcely perceptible at first" which would soon rise until "the Prairies are on fire."

And, he went on, "Now, my friend, I hope you will look ahead beyond the beginning, until your imagination warms in the blaze that I hope to see you kindle. If such fuel as I am able to furnish, will help to illumine our Western world, I will occasionally bestow it."

It was the beginning of a friendship and a flow of illuminating articles that would continue for more than a decade, and which would do much to give the new paper national standing early in its career.

Primitive attempt at check rowing in the planting of corn, used on the prairies in the middle 1850's, invented by Randall S. Jones of Winnebago county, Illinois. From *The Prairie Farmer*, February, 1854.

CHAPTER VI

"This Bewitching Western Life"

F AR too astute to antagonize the great mass of possible subscribers by warning them that he was out to reform their way of life, the young editor began the formal issue of his paper in January, 1841, with subtle, not frontal attacks. Instead of declaring that small diversified farms would be more profitable than careless beef-growing, he published wood-cuts and columns of description of the Ayrshire dairy cows, of which there were none in Illinois. Admitting that stock-raising was always to be important on the prairies, he offered to publish free the pedigrees of blooded stock if farmers would send them in.

He printed nothing about the social necessity of breaking and tilling the public range, but he did announce that the Union Agricultural Society would try out new farm implements for six months to see if they fit the needs of the West, "where the hoe is so little used, because of the scarcity of labor." If the test were successful, the Society planned to buy the patent rights and manufacture the implements for the Society members at cost.

Wright's opening gun against the lack of a "poor man's fence" was not a blast at the timber monopolists, but a suggestion that a plant, unknown to the prairie farmers, the Osage orange, which was said to grow in Arkansas, might well prove to be the thing. "It would be a great favor to have an account of it furnished us."

He relegated the Educational Department to the back page, Page 8, and limited its content to short calls for readers to demand that the Legislature spend the $122,000 in the College and Seminary Funds for a Normal School, and to organize auxiliaries to the newly formed Illinois State Educational Society, so that public discussions might be given the needs for the Normal, and the appointment of a Superintendent of Common Schools. He asked "whether it be advisable to pass laws levying direct taxes to sustain common schools."

"There is," he wrote amiably enough, "no absolute necessity that auxiliary societies be organized in order to have discussions and addresses, but it seems to be the fashion of the day to have everything accomplished by means of societies."

But even with this canny restraint of his enthusiasm for school reform, he found he had frightened some of his trustees. Among them were men who shared his belief that agricultural and school progress were essentially one and the same, but there were others who regarded the presence of even a meager half column of back-page school news in the January and March issues as likely to scare off farm subscribers. Schools made men think of taxes.

For the sake of the paper's success Wright dropped the educational column and turned to whipping up enthusiasm for the Society's Cattle Show and Fair, drummed up memberships, and was rewarded by seeing citizens in three counties—Lake, Kendall and DuPage—join the Society, raising to eight the counties represented. With spring, the number of correspondents grew. The Yankee progressives —many of them physicians who, as a frontier class were articulate upon scientific agriculture and horticulture— wrote long and well for the paper. Until June the volume of mail arriving on the editor's desk grew so steadily that Wright began to regard his earlier dreams as too modest. It seemed that the paper would reach, sooner than he had expected, the ideal—a journal devoted wholly to Western agriculture, filled entirely with "original matter" and turning its back squarely upon the Eastern agricultural press which must necessarily devote itself to its local problems of old, "worn-out" soil.

As the year 1841 went on, Wright moved cautiously, so far as editorial fiat was concerned, preferring to let letter writers stir up controversy and discussion. A genius at enticing his readers to unburden themselves in his columns, and at recognizing in his mail the letters which would most interest his subscribers, he was an instantaneous success as an editor, but his preoccupation with a thousand and one "causes" and items of public interest, handicapped him severely as a publisher. By June he discovered that his estimate of the cost of the paper, printers and engravers was going to fall a good $400 short. Hard times held down the subscriptions to a scant 500.

His carelessness about detail and his fondness for spending time in excited, visionary conversation about the future of the West or the needs of schools and agriculture, had caused delays in getting earlier numbers to the subscribers. Now, in June, he met serious trouble when the printer, after running off the copies on the first of the month, refused to let Wright have them until an item of $20 was paid. As Wright explained it later to his readers, "We waited along till the last of the month in hopes of effecting a compromise; and then, seeing no prospects of it, got out an 'extra' explaining the cause of the delay, which was sent to every subscriber."

He had then dispatched an order to New York for type, intending to print the issue himself, and had laid out the copy for the new printer to set, as soon as the type should arrive. Thereupon, as he confessed, he had airily set out upon "a tour into the country, to see how the farmers felt about the paper."

On his return to Chicago, "instead of finding the number

all ready for the press, as was expected, the type had not come, the order not having been correctly prepared; or rather a stipulation on our part having been inserted which should have been left out."

In desperation he had next sent to Buffalo for type, only to be told that the order could not be filled inside of four or five weeks. At this juncture he had had the paper printed on the only substitute available, old, worn type for which he apologized abjectly.

Just how belated the July issue was, he never said, although a subscriber at nearby Michigan City was complaining on August 20 that he hadn't yet received it.

Wright admitted that the delay had seriously harmed the paper since so many subscribers felt sure they had been duped. A good half dozen other agricultural papers in the

"This farmer has a mortal abhorrence of all books and papers which relate to his business;" illustration for an article "The Unlucky Farmer" in *The Prairie Farmer*, August, 1848.

West had recently collapsed and farm journalism had been given a black eye.

There was "a sad falling off in communications," and when the July issue made its tardy appearance, it carried Wright's admission that he had given up all thought of receiving the $300 in salary which he had expected, and that he was therefore giving his editorial services free for the year.

Within a few weeks, however, he was off for the East, not to return for six weeks, again leaving copy to be set, fortunately with success. Probably this trip, like so many of his journeys to the East in succeeding years was for conferences with Horace Mann, Secretary of the Massachusetts Board of Education, and the most notable advocate of common schools. Home he came in time to sound in the September issue a tribute, both ringing and humorous, to the West: "We are once more at home, after an

"The Mixed Up Farmer" illustration for article in the March, 1849, "Prairie Farmer," pointing out to settlers the need for digging wells, planting shade trees and flowers, sheltering livestock and storing wheat in barns.

absence of about six weeks; and glad we are again to enter upon the delightful duties connected with this paper. The East has charms to make a limited period pass pleasantly; though a residence of nine years in the West most woefully obliterates one's affection for it, even if it be the land of one's birth." He advised any young man who, having emigrated to the West, sighed for a return to the East, to go back there "and, if within six months he were not tenfold more homesick for the West, he would be one of a thousand." To any young husband whose wife complained about having given up father and mother and an Eastern home for a hard life in the Western wilds, he suggested that she be sent back "with the understanding when she leaves that she shall not return for three or six months.

"He will soon receive letters wishing he were with her; then wishing for an opportunity to return with some friend; then urging him to come for her; and finally telling him if he does not come soon she shall start for home alone. But keep her away till the fixed time for her return, and she will not be so urgent to leave again for many a day.

"There is something most bewitching in this Western life."

His dash to the East was merely a longer version of his dashes down-State on subscription tours, or, what was more disturbing to the business of publishing, on common-school crusades. There were times when, after talking long into the night with farmer hosts, far out on the prairies, he rode off in the morning forgetting the list which contained the names of subscribers. Then there was, most likely, another delay in the issuance of the next number.

Hard times still clouded the sky. A distressing number of farmers in the fields, or farmers' wives at cabin doors, told him they couldn't afford the $1.00 for his paper, or, worse, they wrote their names in the book then never paid. With Chicago print shops still in the primitive stage, compositors let the difficulties of reading the stiff penmanship of farmers lead them into double error.

What helped the paper to weather the storm in its first year was the young editor's willingness to confess his faults and blunders in print. He took his readers into his confidence about the paper's finances, its troubles, how he had been cheated on the quality of paper stock—"it being much lighter than the sample shown us," and in the December issue he told how he had been forced to resort to "the disagreeable labor of 'shinning'([1]) almost every number to pay the printer."

The financial crisis had been so bad, he said, that he had not only forgotten about making anything for himself, but he had been forced to produce $400 from his own pocket to keep the paper afloat. He was trying to earn a living on the side, having inserted in the paper an advertisement "Stoves for Sale" in behalf of himself and his brother Timothy. The latter had designed a farm cottage, and made the drawing, himself, all quite complete, for the September issue.

When in Chicago, Wright spent many evenings at the office, 112 Lake Street, where he maintained a "Farmers' Reading Room," keeping for their benefit "when they come to town on business" books on agriculture and some thirty-three agricultural periodicals with which he "exchanged."

Digging into his own scanty funds he got enough money to start the second year with an increase of from eight to twelve pages, and promised "to make up for our lack of competency, so far as possible, by increased and persevering efforts, and to issue the paper, henceforth,

(1) By *shinning*, in mercantile phrase, is meant running about to one's acquaintances, to borrow money to meet the emergency of a note at the bank. It is doubtless so called because, in the great hurry of picking up cash to meet the hour of three, which perchance is just at hand, the borrower, not having the fear of wheelbarrows, boxes, barrels, piles of brick, etc., before his eyes, is very apt to run furiously against them with his shins.
—Bartlett's Dictionary of Americanisms.

on the first of the month without fail." His appeals stirred into action many farmers who had, for all the vexing delays and moments of doubt, acquired a feeling that, somehow, this strange editor was a personal friend. Communications in 1842 rose, and so did subscriptions. More than 200 letters were published and advertising increased from three or four small insertions to more than half a page.

One letter, containing a suggestion worth incalculable amounts to the paper, arrived in February of that second year—1842. It was the proposal from "Incog," (later to be revealed as Dr. M. L. Knapp of LaPorte, Indiana) that the name, *The Union Agriculturalist and Western Prairie Farmer*, be shortened. "Simply The Prairie Farmer would have been better," he said.

This proposal was praised by another correspondent in the June issue, and with the July number, Wright announced that next year, the name would be adopted, and the size of the journal changed from small newspaper size to large octavo, with 32 pages. Times were improving and the paper was catching hold. The older agricultural papers of the East had published high praise of the lively new Western monthly, and Wright was mailing more than 100 copies of each issue to subscribers in the Atlantic seaboard states. In the August number he declared that from the way things looked it would pay its own expenses for the year, but in private he was dissatisfied. For two years he had toiled without any financial return, and with, indeed, an actual cash outlay of his own part, and still he was forbidden to get out the kind of paper he wished. The ban on school news defeated his major interest.

The time for a show-down was to come on October 19 and 20 when the trustees of the Union Agricultural Society met at Aurora, Illinois, for their annual meeting. The sessions were to be held at this time and place for the convenience of the members who would be attending the Society's Cattle Show and Fair—which Wright had publicized in the paper and in personal interviews.

Wright had his guns loaded and when the Society convened, he, as secretary, began firing. It was, he said, to be confidently expected that the paper would soon be recognized as *the* agricultural paper for the man who tilled the prairies, but the expense for the two years had come to around $2,300, and the receipts to $1,535.84. There had been a loss of $117.66 during the year on depreciated bank paper and some 300 of last year's subscribers had failed to pay. If the paper continued, as he hoped it would, new type should be bought at a cost of $350. As a matter of fact, Wright blandly announced, he had already sent for the type, though, of course, if the trustees didn't care to back him up, "it shall be sold without being unpacked." The changes in format, proposed for the coming year, would help the paper. The cost of publishing it in 1843 would be around $1,265.

The Mechanics' Institute, an organization of laborers and skilled workmen in Chicago whose attempt to create a library Wright had supported, proposed supporting the

MECHANICAL DEPARTMENT.
JOHN GAGE, Editor.

Symbolizing the New Western Movement for the union of farmers and laborers, this heading was introduced by Wright in January, 1843 above *The Prairie Farmer's* Mechanical Department News.

paper if they could supervise four pages of each issue.

This sudden mingling of the interests of the industrial artisan with those of the farmer who prided himself upon living independent of toil in shops and cities, ran counter to the ideas of some of the trustees, but not so much as did the next subject into which Wright, reading from the speaker's stand, now launched.

"It is also in contemplation," said he, "to add an educational department. The subject of common school education being one of such vital importance to the permanent welfare of our State, there should be a means employed by which the people at large would be awakened to its attention."

There must have been a rustling among the trustees at this point. Here Wright was back just where he had been in March, 1842, when they had compelled him to drop the educational department and keep the paper hewing to the line of practical agriculture.

"No more effectual means can be employed," he continued, "than the public press, and as it will be difficult, if not impossible, to sustain a publication exclusively devoted to this subject, it would seem most desirable . . . to have such a department added to The Prairie Farmer. . . . It is desirable to have such articles first appear in a publication not connected with a political party, as most of our political papers are. . . . It will be far less expensive to add a few pages to the Society's paper than to publish a separate organ. . . . By far the most important consideration (is) a much greater number will be enabled to obtain the educational matter. . . . Very many will subscribe to an agricultural paper who would be unable or unwilling to subscribe to one devoted merely to education. It is the farmers—the people at large—who need to be reached and aroused to that exertion which is required of them in consideration of the vast importance of furnishing their children with a good common school education."

But he did not propose to "occupy any part of the 24 pages" with educational news. "Some have objected to the articles under this head that have already appeared, preferring the matter should be altogether agricultural. In consequence, nothing more has been said upon education." But it was possible that the State Educational Society would raise the funds to support the increase of eight pages.

DEVOTED TO WESTERN AGRICULTURE, MECHANICS AND EDUCATION.

Vol. III. CHICAGO, JANUARY, 1843. No. 1.

JOHN S. WRIGHT, Editor.
OFFICE, 112 LAKE STREET, CHICAGO, ILLINOIS.

ADVERTISEMENTS inserted square or under, first insertion dollar; subsequent o will be counted r early advr ... wing terms: for one nts; second, one han one square m.

fast receiving new names. Of the wisdom of this course there can be no doubt; for if the paper be more valuable to one farmer than another, it is certainly to that one who is in straitened circumstances, who, being unable to test useless experiments, needs the advice an uce of others. It is the poor man, too, who most fee animal, and therefore more h re of the var

Wright hammered ahead, carrying the fight straight to the opposition. He demanded that "these three congenial subjects—agriculture, education and mechanics—be united in The Prairie Farmer, and it will become a paper of which the society—every Western farmer—yes, every Western citizen, may be proud. ... Above all things let us be united."

In private conversation with the trustees, as in subsequent issues of the paper, he pointed out that he had worked for the Society and the paper for two years without salary; and had, moreover, advanced some $400 from his own bankrupt pocket to keep the paper going.

The upshot was that he came away from the meeting
the sole owner of the paper. He was re-elected recording
and corresponding secretary for another year, and continued to promote the Society, drum up members and
foster it as before. What had evidently decided the trustees to transfer the paper to him were three factors—the
debt owed him, the failure of the paper to support itself,
and the doubts of many as to its future, if, as seemed certain, there were no way to prevent Wright from crowding
the pages with all this controversial, radical talk of higher
taxes for common schools.

In effect, Wright had told the trustees to raise more
money for the paper or allow him to run it as he pleased.
And the trustees had chosen the easier and more amicable
path of washing their hands of the paper's finances altogether. However one of them, the energetic and progressive James T. Gifford of Juliet, gave him $15 toward the
purchase of the new type and others said they would help.

Back in Chicago Wright penned strong articles on education for the December issue, urged the State Educational
Society to move quickly so that it might have the eight
extra pages, and wrote an editorial boldly attacking that
Sacred Ark of the conservatives, the protective tariff.
Born a Whig and, like so many of the emigrants from
New England, still maintaining loyalty to that party, he
nevertheless had come a long way toward Jacksonian Democracy of the West since he had begun to study farm problems. In September, when he had been subject to the
wishes of the trustees, he had written for the October issue
four columns generally favoring the tariff bill which the
Whigs in Congress were preparing to pass. Questioning
some points gingerly, he agreed, however, with the principle that the protective tariff was a beneficence to the
farmer. A protective tariff, he said, was "the American
system." But two months later, when he had become his

own master he wrote for the December issue, "The truth is, we had been itching to say something about the tariff and were only withheld by fear of giving offense to some of our subscribers. . . . We greatly fear we overrated the protection afforded to the wool grower . . . the farmers have been grossly humbugged by the late tariff . . . and we incline to the opinion that in all essential particulars the recent tariff law has been passed for the benefit of manufacturers and at the expense of the farmers. . . . And if the manufacturers suppose the farmers are to sit down and suck their thumbs under such one-sided legislation, they will find out their mistake when perhaps it will be too late. What could they do in Congress with the whole farming interest opposed to them?"

With the January number the Mechanical Department, under a drawn heading which showed the farmer and mechanic striking hands, began filling its four pages, with Wright, himself, editing it, since John Gage, the miller who had agreed to conduct the department, had been called temporarily away. Wright dealt with inventions and practical subjects, avoiding the charge that his policy would be to unite the farmers and laborers in a class group.

But he featured prominently an address the Indiana reformer, Dr. M. L. Knapp, soon to move to Chicago to help launch Rush Medical College, had made at the Aurora meeting in October—a speech that bombarded the opponents of the democratic plan for the prairies.

The doctor said, "I would say, then, to those who deplore want of moral power and elevated rank in the agricultural producing class, that the work of reform must begin in the schoolhouse. Agreeably to the last census, one-seventeenth part of the white population of Illinois, over twenty years of age, can neither read nor write. Were the record to include natives only, and descend to the age of ten years, the proportion would be lamentably increased.... Why is education so neglected? Why is there such a squandering of the children's substance? Where are the neat and comfortable schoolhouses that should adorn the thousands of districts where common schools are demanded throughout the State? Where are the normal schools ... the high schools and academies ... the colleges? Where is the enthusiasm that should pervade all classes on these momentous subjects?"

He voiced the reformers' argument that so long as farmers were forced by law to fence in their crops against the raids of wandering livestock, the settlement of the prairies would be slow, and common schools scanty.

Launching the January, 1843, issue as coming from "John S. Wright, Editor, Office 112 Lake St., Chicago" instead of "Published by the Union Agricultural Society; Edited by the Corresponding Secretary," Wright said "We expect to make something out of the paper, but think it is to our permanent advantage to use up the receipts for a year or two in its improvement." For the present he gave his readers his pledge that he would take no more than $200 a year, since the help he had received from so many of the most influential men in the West obligated him to show "a corresponding disinterestedness."

It was February before Wright, himself, could cut loose on schools. Part of January he had to spend in Springfield, acting as secretary of the Illinois State Agricultural Society. The body had never done anything more than adopt a constitution and elect officers, but the incessantly active secretary was bound it should go, and taking advantage of his authority to issue a report, sent one out, describing how the Union Agricultural Society was showing the way. Some 7,000 people had attended its Cattle Show and Fair at Aurora last October. It had started *The Prairie Farmer;* was planning to establish an experimental farm "and by and by, an agricultural school." Nineteen counties had organized agricultural societies and most of them had held fairs. "More than two-fifths of the population of Illinois are embraced within the limits of agricultural societies."

He forebore to boast that his paper's encouragement had had much to do with the organizing of these county societies and fairs. But it had done so and it could have been said that he and his paper were among the chief factors that would enable statisticians to announce, a decade later, that Illinois stood first among all the states in number and activity of county agricultural societies.

When he got down to work on the school question, in the March issue, he began softly, pointing out the various views on what should be done, and urging all factions to send him their views. In announcing the formation of a Farmers' Club, to be held every Thursday evening in *The Prairie Farmer* office at 112 Lake Street, Chicago, he listed topics that were purely agricultural. He was cannily moving to get the attention of farmers before working the conversation around, as he inevitably would, to the need for higher taxation to obtain better schools.

There was shrewdness, too, in the leading article he published under the heading, "Educational Department," in the April number—shrewdness in appealing to the anti-clerical, anti-aristocratic, French Republican bias which so many Westerners had acquired from the long dominant political ideals of Thomas Jefferson.

"The necessity of education," this article read, "will be admitted by all; and here in the West, for years to come, it must chiefly be obtained by common schools. In the most favored States, where academies, high schools, colleges, etc., most abound, not a fifth part of the children and youth are instructed in them; even there the great majority receive their education in the common schools. The new States cannot expect, with many years' labor, to possess the advantages of the older ones, and, for a long

period, common schools will furnish the only practicable
plan for education for at least nine-tenths of the children.
. . . Republicanism and ignorance are incompatible, and,
when it is remembered that, in Illinois, one in seventeen
over twenty years of age can neither read nor write, it
would seem high time for our public men to be adopting
measures to stem the tide of ignorance which threatens
to engulf us. . . . Thousands of foreigners locate amongst
us annually, who are utterly ignorant of our language. . . .
For them, common schools furnish the only available
means of educating their children. . . .

"Now the education of the people is the best, and in
fact the only, antidote to the sway of a domineering
priesthood; without it, any people will sooner or later be
brought to recognize no law superior to that of the priest.
And, in our opinion, Calvinist though we be, it matters little whether the priest be papist or protestant; time and opportunity will make both alike ambitious and overbearing.
There is no dependence, other than upon the intelligence
of the people, for the preservation of either civil or
religious liberty."

Wright had earned the right to speak thus freely without being charged with any anti-Catholicism. Both he and
his father had shown active friendship for the first
Catholic church in Chicago, and Wright had, during 1841-
42, put his paper on record as welcoming any number of
European immigrants to the prairies—a declaration that
ran counter to the tide of bigotry that was rising, and
which would, by 1844, produce in New York political agitation for an "American" movement. He had given prominence in his columns to the reformer Dr. Knapp's demand
that the prairies work to attract those "whole villages that
were leaving Europe"; such people "with their sterling
virtues of economy and industry" were needed in the West.

As his pen warmed to its work of preparing his April,

1843, editorial on common schools, Wright grew angry at politicians. "Why should there not be an educational convention held, and the attendance of delegates solicited from every county in the State? Both political parties can hold convention after convention, print their miserable party trash by the cartload, send their emissaries in all directions, and neither labor nor expense is considered; but let a proposition be made to call a convention to deliberate upon education, or to raise means to circulate information concerning it by the press, or to appoint only one man to the whole State to visit the several counties, and lecture upon it, besides performing other important duties, and the cry of poverty is raised, 'The people, the dear people, are unable to bear the expense.'

"This spring a convention will probably be held by each political party in the seven new congressional districts, to nominate candidates for Congress, and surely the importance of the cause of education will warrant the holding of one convention by its friends, and we shall hope to see one called. Peoria would be a suitable place if it could be appointed before the close of navigation—say, in October. . . . We should like an expression of opinion with regard to it."

He came back to the failure of the Legislature at its last session to create the office of Superintendent of Common Schools. The voters had not sent in the petitions he had mailed them. "The chief reason was the dislike to ask for the creation of another office, under the present embarrassment of the State treasury. . . . Now it had been considered that the expense, say $1,200 per annum, would be only about $13 to a county and not a single dollar to a school district, very few would have refused their signatures."

He had arranged for a lecturer, at that time, to enlighten the legislators, but the solons hadn't attended, and the campaign had failed. The only hope still lay in the people.

Instead of crippling the paper as the conservative trustees had feared, the volume of school propaganda had aided, perhaps saved it. In the May issue Wright revealed that he had hired "a well-educated man, a fine writer, bred a farmer, fond of agricultural pursuits and industrious to start editing the paper in June. The new man would allow Wright to travel the prairies and campaign for school reform. "The improvement of common schools—the establishment of a good system with one or more superintendents, we intend shall be so united with The Prairie Farmer as to make them mutually sustain each other."

With the June issue the identity of the "Associate Editor" was revealed—J. Ambrose Wight, the New Englander who had operated "Deacon" Wright's store on the Rock River until the Deacon's death in 1840. With the close of the store, Wight had moved to a farm near Rockford, whence, during 1841, he had sent his friend John S. Wright letters on farm subjects. Early in 1842 he had become editor of the *Winnebago Forum*, a small venture which proved, however, too large to be supported by the scattering population, and in 1843 Wight was wondering how to make ends meet when the offer came to edit *The Prairie Farmer*.

Accepting promptly, Ambrose Wight had by December shown such capacity for organization and such comprehension of John A. Wright's ideas that the owner, after a trip through the prairies, came home and announced he was "leaving for New York and Washington for three weeks." Illness and hard work on the Third Annual Cattle Show of the Union Agricultural Society, had worn Wright down. Besides, he needed to see what the educational reformers of the East were doing. He felt secure, his paper's circulation had reached 2,000 a month.

CHAPTER VII

"No Highways of Ignorance"

J. AMBROSE WIGHT not only bettered the paper editorially, he added a business efficiency which John S. Wright had not taken, or would not take the time to apply. In February, 1844, a new system of "club-subscriptions," selling the paper at seventy-seven cents to any group of thirteen annual subscribers, was introduced and helped shoot the circulation forward so rapidly that by April, anywhere from thirty to forty new names were being added each day, the total number of copies to be printed that month reaching 3,360.

Wright at last was free to give all his energies to common schools. Ambrose Wight had brought him the one thing he wanted most, escape from business detail, and the opportunity to let his imagination wing into desired heavens.

From the East, where he was studying common schools that April, and where he obtained ammunition for his campaign from the sensational Massachusetts Board of Education reports by Horace Mann, Wright sent back to his paper two articles which, when published in the May issue, gave both him and his paper unquestioned leadership in the Western educational movement.

In one of the articles he returned to his plea made the previous year for an educational convention at some central point, such as Peoria. He had gotten nowhere with it in 1843, but now he declared it imperative, since the Legislature would be asked, very insistently, to take action at its coming session, and a definite program must be

worked out for the solons to consider. He named Peoria
as the site of the convention, and Wednesday, October 9, as
the day. All communities were invited to send delegates.

The strategy of the campaign for a new school law was
obvious in the second of his articles, which was headed
"Common Schools vs. Academies." It was to be a continu-
ation of the policy he had touched the year before—an
assault upon private schools as the enemies of the public
schools, and was astutely keyed to the political hour.
Four years earlier, Wright had seen the voters of the
West and of the nation rise to the Whig's plea that an honest and simple farmer of the West be elected President in
place of a wealthy, fashionable and aristocratic Easterner.
They had elected Harrison by the expedient of stealing
the traditional appeal of the Jacksonian Democrats, who
had long ruled by convincing the electorate that they
alone represented the masses in their eternal struggle
with the classes.

Himself the product of private schools and, indeed, the
builder of Chicago's first, and private, school, Wright had
as a prairie dweller, undergone a pronounced change. Intimate contact with the Western farmers had turned him
from faith in the privately endowed colleges and schools
of which his beloved uncle, Chester Dewey, was so bright
a flower. Such institutions in the West were a bane and
not a blessing, because their very existence prevented
common schools from ever getting started.

He had even thrown off enough New England prejudice
to enable him to understand the Southern-born who
inhabited lower Illinois, and who looked with growing
resentment upon the way the bustling, coercive Yankees
were reaching down from the northern part of the State
to take over the whole commonwealth. The Kentuckians,
Virginians and Tennesseeans who had settled Southern
Illinois had been fed on the gospel that all Yankees were

skin-flints, money sharpers, sellers of wooden nutmegs, stealers of slaves, practitioners of free love and aetheism.

The more ignorant of these Border Staters believed that "schools were Yankee tricks, where sly cunning was taught"[1] and that a man was a fool to send his children to school to learn more than his father knew. Among the intelligent were those who held that while schools were to be desired, Yankee schools were not, and anything educational proposed by the immigrants of northern Illinois must be an extension of the New England civilization.

Straight to the heart of these masses went Wright's pen when he announced that after long questioning of the matter, he had concluded that academies and select schools created "erroneous distinctions between children" since they often excluded good scholars and admitted blockheads merely "because the parents of one are poor and the other rich." Poor children had to suffer since "an ignoramus, because he attends *the academy*, will strut and swell and lord it over his humble playmate attending the common school. . . . This is wrong. Children should be made to feel that true excellence consists in moral and intellectual worth, and the distinctions of property should be kept out of view as far as possible. They will learn fast enough on this point without extra effort to instruct them. . . . If the wealthy and influential portions of a community establish a select school, withdrawing their aid from the common school, the latter will . . . decline in interest. A few towns in the West may be able to sustain one or more schools, together with good common schools; but in the most of our towns and settlements they would prove the ruin of the latter." The Legislature was chartering so many academies that a halt must be called.

Repeating his slogan, "Education is a public good," he offered as a substitute for the academies which did, he

(1) Letter from W. B. in *Prairie Farmer,* July, 1855.

admitted, often give superior instruction, a new system of graded schools, supported by public taxation. Instead of sending large and small children to one school, "the schools should be divided, classifying the scholars according to their progress. Where the number of scholars would admit of it, there should be at least three grades of schools. For the small children, say under ten years of age, female teachers should be employed, and the schools should be as numerous as possible, to facilitate attendance. For the next grade, the instruction and number of schools should depend upon circumstances. For the highest grade there should be but one school within a circuit of three miles diameter, no matter how thickly settled the town . . . and generally there should be but one school to a township. . . . Instead of dividing the school as attendance increased, the number of teachers should be increased, giving to each a department as he was best qualified to instruct in."

It was the discovery of this in the yellowing files of *The Prairie Farmer* that led W. L. Pillsbury, the historian of Illinois' schools, to say, in 1886, "Here is a suggestion for graded schools when there was not a graded school in the State."[2] Others would later see in Wright's proposal the first advocacy of what was to become the West's system of township high schools.

Wright went on, in his May editorial, to say that as the scholars graduated from grade to grade, "The teachers, too, would receive certificates for instruction in schools of a certain grade, and would as strongly desire advancement as the scholars . . . and excellent teachers would be constantly preparing for the highest grade of schools."

"This," concluded Pillsbury, "is the first mention that I have seen of a State teacher's certificate."

(2) Early Education in Illinois, W. L. Pillsbury; 16th Biennial Report, Supt. Public Instruction of State of Illinois 1884-86.

Coming home to Illinois, Wright spent the summer of 1844 promoting the "Peoria Convention" as it was destined to be called. Riding the State from end to end, he spoke in halls, barns, homes, groves, log school houses, churches, wherever he could assemble an audience. He published monthly the names of the delegates as communities chose them, and he recorded with pride the names of politicians as they fell into line. Governor Thomas Ford promised to be there. Isaac N. Arnold, a leading Democrat of Chicago, took to the stump, orating for the cause. Steadily Wright pleaded with local newspapers over the State to reprint his "Call", and in September announced that nearly all of them had come out strongly in favor of the convention.

His home town chose some of its most prominent citizens as delegates: John H. Kinzie, who was a member of Chicago's oldest family, Arnold, Mark Skinner, F. C. Sherman, J. Y. Scammon, Dr. Levi D. Boone. There were between 50 and 60 influential men from the State on the floor when the Peoria Convention assembled on October 9. Wright called the meeting to order, read his ideas of what should be asked of the Legislature.

It was, generally speaking, a thoroughly organized school system which Wright proposed to the Convention, and eight committees were appointed to consider the various branches of his paper.

Although his reading of the plan had been a lengthy one, the delegates, at its conclusion, hadn't had enough, and invited him to speak again at 7:00 P. M. the next night. As the master spirit of the occasion, he was in his element. When, during the debates, objections were raised to this point or that, it was Wright who could make answer, citing Eastern precedents, repeating what he had learned during his many talks with Horace Mann and other educational authorities of New England.

When the committees made their reports, the Con-

vention unanimously adopted a resolution urging the
Legislature to create the office of State Superintendent,
who would visit the schools, examine teachers and issue
honorary certificates to the meritorious, qualifying them
to teach in any school of the State. It also resolved to
make each township a school district governed by three
elected trustees, and to make it possible for any six citizens in a township to secure, upon demand, a local election upon the question of taxing property to support
schools.

Named with two other delegates to put these demands
into a memorial and present it to the Legislature, Wright
left the convention with a unanimous vote of thanks ringing in his ears. On the way back to Chicago he stopped
at settlements to make speeches on the need for popular
pressure on the Legislature, and he issued a call for another convention—one of "teachers, parents and others"
to be held in the State House at Springfield on January 9,
1845, to form a new State Educational Society, the original having winked out without ever having done anything
about the plan of raising money to support Wright's paper.

So busy was he, across the next months, drumming up
sentiment for the meeting and persuading settlers to write
their Legislators, that when the time came to present the
Memorial to the solons, he didn't have it written. However, his pen was at its best when pushed for time, and on
the eve of the hearing before the joint committees on
Schools and Education, at Springfield, he sat down and
poured himself into the work.

It was a paper that would take hours to read that he
carried in his hands as he took the rostrum in the Legislative hall and faced his listeners. First he read the plan
for official organization, then suddenly and bluntly brought
the politicians up to the one thing in the whole program
that troubled them most—taxation.

"We come out frankly and boldly," said Wright, "and acknowledge the whole system—every effort—is intended only as a means of allurement to draw the people into the grasp of this most awful monster—*a school tax*.

"But start not back in alarm. After all, he may not be so terrible as some have perhaps imagined. Used with skill and judgment, and no other power can accomplish what he will; no other can work such changes in your common schools . . ." What, he asked were the alternatives to a tax on public property? The income from the school, college and seminary funds would produce only 34 cents a year for each of the 150,000 children between five and seventeen years of age. The difference could be made up by the parents of school children, but this would "grind to dust" a large portion of the population, or it would force the poor to keep their children out of school altogether.

Why should the parents of children be forced to support the schools which brought, by their very presence, such increase to the wealth of a community?

"Let the expense for this, as for other public objects, fall where it belongs—upon the property throughout the State. Any other method of compelling support is unequal —most unjust. . . . Suppose all means of education in Illinois were abandoned; who would live here—who purchase property? . . . To construct roads and bridges, property in the vicinity is assessed no matter who is the owner, and it is considered equitable. The fact of the owner's residing a thousand miles distant, and that he never saw the improvement, and probably never will, has no influence."

Wright was now rapidly disarming those legislators from lower Illinois who thought of the Yankees from the Northern part of the State as representatives of the land speculators of New England.

"Why," he persisted, "is it less equitable to assess property to sustain a cause of such paramount importance as the education of the people? Better far that the prairie sloughs should be left unworked, that the poor should beg from door to door, than that no highways of ignorance should be left unfilled, and the children become pigmies of men for lack of the bread of knowledge . . .

"A very large amount of land is owned by non-residents . . . who talk finely of the glories of education, and promise largely, yet they are a long way off, and might disappoint our hopes" if support of education were to be voluntary. "There is a way by which we can make sure of their proportion . . . make all pay according to their property."

Not only the New England States but Pennsylvania, Ohio, Indiana, Kentucky and Missouri had school taxes. Illinois should listen to "the strong language of experience."

"It is safe to trust the majority," he trumpeted.

Then he loosed upon the private schools a righteous wrath that carried him far beyond anything he had ever written about them in his *Prairie Farmer*.

"And here permit us to say one word upon the propriety and necessity of discountenancing the erection of those nurseries of pomposity and contemptible vanity, yclept 'select schools' or academies. They may be of occasional advantage to individuals, but they are a positive curse to the public in such a population as exists generally in Illinois. They absorb the support which is absolutely essential to the existence of the common school." Whatever might be their advantage "it is at largely increased expense, so that only the more wealthy will avail themselves of it. In consequence, the school by which the great majority are to be educated is left to eke out a sickly existence, if indeed it exist at all . . . when the same expense and labor given to it, which is given from nothing but foolish vanity to the 'select school', would make the former nearly as good for the children of the wealthy, besides furnishing the same means of education to numbers equally as worthy."

Halt the wholesale chartering of private schools, he begged; start devoting energy and means to the common schools and the latter would commence an onward march which would in time perfect a system that allowed the pupil to go from the elementary grades up to college.

"Then," said Wright, "the child of the cottage and the palace shall meet on terms of perfect equality."

So well did Wright answer the questions of the Joint Committee that the Chairman of the Senate group W. W. Thompson, wrote to the *Galena Gazette* praising the farm editor's efficiency in "explaining and elucidating the splendid system,"[3] and Senator Constable from the Wabash River country rose from his desk to tell his fellow committeemen that "it was the best thing he ever saw or heard upon the subject."[4]

Thompson soon presented the Memorial to the Senate where Constable moved that 10,000 copies be printed and distributed to the voters. Wright heard "not a voice" raised against the motion, but saw Lieutenant-Governor John Moore "so afraid of Yankee-school innovations that he pettishly declared the motion lost."[5]

A second motion was made to print 5,000 and was carried unanimously.

The Memorial's demands were incorporated in a bill for which Wright lobbied strenuously as it wound its way to a final vote. When the law at length appeared, Wright declared in his paper that while it was "by no means what many of the friends of education desired, yet it is a decided improvement upon the old one," Pillsbury, in his judging of the law forty years later, de-

(3) Ibid. (4) In Memoriam: John S. Wright, by Augustine W. Wright.
(5) Ibid.

clared it had brought "substantial progress' to the schools.

The Secretary of State had been made ex-officio Super-intendent of common schools, the township was made the unit of school activity with its three trustees or the county superintendent empowered to examine and certificate teachers as well as to buy sites for schools and libraries without authority from the voters. "A homeopathic dose of taxation was also permitted." It would take not a majority but two-thirds of the voters to demand the levy of a school tax, and even then the tax could not exceed fifteen cents on the hundred dollars worth of property.

This, said Wright in a report to *The Prairie Farmer*, proved that the Legislators were still "too fearful of trust in the majority"; however, he felt "it is very desir-able that all who believe in this method of supporting schools, should give it an immediate trial, and by and by the law may be altered." He thought it incredible "that so many judicious men still doubt the expediencey of taxing property for the purposes of education."

Knowing how few would be the voters who would read the long act, he indexed it, sitting up nights in taverns and private homes, as he drove back to Chicago from Springfield. He advertised that the new school law, with his index and explanatory notes appended, would be sold in pamphlet form at 8 cents each or 20 for $1. He care-fully digested the act for his *Prairie Farmer* subscrib-ers and in the June, 1845, issue declared "If one-half is done than can be under the law as it is, great will be the improvement in our schools. We want a good law, to be sure, but we want action more. Yes, we want action, Action, ACTION; and this you *farmers* must give. . . . Why is the mind—the immortal mind—cared for so little, compared with the body?"

In that same issue of his paper he admitted that he had been "taken to task" for his Memorial's strong words against select schools, but added that he had meant every one of them. "We are not in the habit of considering the value of mind—educated mind—dependent upon the length of the parent's purse. Those who do may advocate the establishment of one set of schools for the rich and another for the poor." He said the public could and should support its own schools.

In place of philanthropy, the West now beheld the spectacle of "some half a dozen wealthy men financing an academy because they thought it would 'build up their town'." The first move, he observed, "is to get a charter for the Big Dough-head Academy ... then all the more wealthy families think they must send to it or they will be charged with penuriousness; some families in moderate circumstances have the same foolish conceit, and who is left to support the common schools?"

Two-thirds of a century later John Williston Cook, studying the school history of Illinois, concluded, "Indeed, Wright seems to have anticipated a large share of the reforms that the last half century has succeeded in accomplishing." (6)

(6) The Educational History of Illinois, by John Williston Cook, 1912.

The wooden husking peg described by an agricultural leader of Illinois, A. Churchill of Kane county, in *The Prairie Farmer* of December, 1843, as a western invention.

CHAPTER VIII

A Bride from Mount Vernon

WHEN Wright had acquired sole control of the paper he had boldly raised the price of advertising fifty per cent, and by the middle of 1845 was able to boast that in both advertising rate and in circulation *The Prairie Farmer* was now ahead of any other paper in the West, with "one or more of the best merchants in almost every town" acting as subscription agents.

In July he printed 5,280 copies and in October declared to his readers that with monthly expenses at "about $215" he expected to make a profit, on the year, of "about $1,100." This he considered "a reasonable sum, for we have worked four years as hard as anybody could without remuneration. . . . We consider The Prairie Farmer, two years hence, printed with 32 pages, good for $2,500 income."

That same October he added an almanac to his publications and in December announced that in January the paper would go to the long hoped-for 32 pages, making it "the equal in size of any agricultural journal in the United States."

The Union Agricultural Society trustees, who had withdrawn from the paper three years before fearing Wright's radicalism would sink it, might now argue that the gradual passing of hard times, and the introduction of a new business system by Ambrose Wight accounted for the paper's success. But they could not deny that in the matter of news purely agricultural, the new managing editor had only followed the lines laid down by John S. Wright in his first two years of sole editorship. The texts still were the need for manuring and liming the black prairie soil, for exchanging the one-crop system to the rotation of crops, for forcing cattlemen, instead of grain-growers, to do the fencing, for fattening blooded stock at home and sending it to the Chicago market instead of selling to migrant drovers on the open range, for planting orchards and shade trees, and for supplanting log cabins with frame dwellings, the plans for which the paper published diligently.

Ambrose Wight had increased the paper's appeal to women by a series of articles describing prairie flowers such as the Fringed Gentian, the Dragon Head, the Phlox, the Partridge Pea, the False Cowslip, the Pucoon, the Blue Spider Wort and the importance of transplanting and preserving them from the plough, but John S. Wright's appeals for schools had stirred them deeply. It had been the fires of controversy kindled in the fight for the common schools that had made the paper so spectacular—a veritable spear-head of a movement that was surging ahead, all over the West.

Forty years later, Pillsbury, the school historian of Illinois, said that Wright "made The Prairie Farmer a most excellent school journal, all the more effective because it reached the patrons of the school more than the teachers. . . . The school history of this period must be largely written from its pages."

School news was not limited by Wright to thundering editorials or discussions of the innumerable educational conventions. He wrote, or printed letters from correspondents on such living themes as teachers "who whipped too much" or desks that were too high for short legs, or the "million illiterates" in the nation, or the 2,000,000 children with no chance to learn reading or writing, or the glib salesmen who bribed or tricked county superintendents into text books that New York had discarded, or the system in which "every pupil had a book different from all the other pupils."

At one of the most important of the many school conventions, the one at Jacksonville, June 23-26, in 1845, he pushed through a resolution urging teachers to subscribe to Horace Mann's *Massachusetts Common School Journal* or Francis Dwight's *District School Journal* in New York. And his hand was seen in the convention's urging of teachers to attend the General State School Convention which was planned for Chicago in the fall of 1846.

By the end of 1845 Wright was stirring with the desire to do something more for common schools than merely to organize conventions, lobby in legislatures and rouse the voters. Ten years before, when still a boy, he had been rich enough to build Chicago's first schoolhouse. Now, at thirty, it was time to do something material again.

"I set conscientiously to work to make some money to use in that sacred cause," was the explanation he later gave for his action in the winter of 1845-6. "Having recovered from the mortification and disgust of being permitted to go to ruin when a wealthy uncle, who had made largely by and through me, could with perfect ease have saved my property without risk," and "having obtained renewed energies and stronger confidence in the future of the West, and of Chicago, by years of cruising and delightful intercourse among the noble hearts of the prairie farmers, I resolved again to make another fortune in Chicago property."

All through the hard times he had kept preaching the manifest destiny of the city and prairies, but now, late in 1845, he felt sure that others must see how imminent it was. Chicago which had only grown from 4,000 to 8,000 between 1836 and '44, was increasing fifty per cent in the year 1845, and would go past 12,000 in population. Wright thought the hour had come, and hurried to New York to try and borrow money for real estate purchases. To his dismay he found there "not the least confidence in Chicago, it having been for ten years a synonym for all that was wild and visionary."

Rich men, who had lost heavily in the 1837 collapse of "The Great Western Land Mania," asked him how Illinois could ever attract heavy immigration or investment so long as its state bonds "were only worth 25 to 20 cents on the dollar, and three years of accrued interest not reckoned?"

No one would lend him money on such a prospect, but he found one capitalist, Frederic Bronson, who would for $30,000, and only $1,000 down, sell him a block "in the heart of Chicago on the river." But Wright was helpless to snatch the bargain. "I had no means to buy with. . . . I could make no one see it."

What he had was leisure—and a pen, the one weapon he knew best how to use. "I wrote a series of fifteen or twenty articles for the *Commercial Advertiser* and the *Evening Post* about the various agricultural products of the West, their profits, etc.", and was able to show "fairly and conclusively that by 1858 or '59, our State would pay her full interest without any increase in the rate of taxation. . . . Though no one would see the future of the West and of Chicago as I did, my own confidence had never been so strong." Digging into statistics to hurl at the Eastern capitalists, he grew more and more excited about the future of Chicago, and coming home in April, 1846, coaxed his brothers, Timothy and Walter, to go his security so that he could buy the Bronson block. It had risen now to $37,000 but he bought it. Ten years later it was worth over $450,000.

Another reason for making money was that he was

engaged to be married that September. With characteristic imagination and optimism and courage, he had not
hesitated to go straight into the drawing rooms of Mount
Vernon, itself, to claim a bride.

The son of a New England tradesman was wooing a
Southern belle, related to many of the First Families of
Virginia, and reared in all the aristocratic ideals and
prejudices of that social caste. She had been served by
slaves; he was the exponent of a democratic ideal which
had kept him for the past ten years battling for "the industrial classes" and for the education of backwoods children at public expense. She came from a civilization which
depended upon the maintenance of society as it was, he
from one which depended upon change, progress, reform.

He was tall, dark-haired, enthusiastic, optimistic, his
eye wide and sparkling blue. She was also blue of eye,
her features though plain were attractive, she had a fine
figure, a sharp wit, a fiery temper—and red hair. She
could claim kinship with not only the Turners and Blackburns, from whom she was descended, but with the Washingtons, Byrds, Corbins and other F. F. V's. Her father,
Henry Smith Turner, at whose mansion, Wheatlands, in
Jefferson county, she had been born, February 29, 1820,
was a planter of social note, and her mother, Catherine
Blackburn Turner, had come of a family, the Blackburns,
which regarded itself as of even higher tone.

At her birth, Catherine Turner's mother had died, leaving her to a niece—Mrs. John Augustine Washington.

The dying mother had been doubly related to the
Washingtons, her older sister Julia having married Bushrod Washington, nephew of the immortal George and in-
heritor of Mount Vernon. Her niece, Jane Blackburn, had
married Bushrod's nephew, John Augustine Washington,
and it had been to this Jane, the dying woman's closest
friend, that the baby girl had been given.

Jane Washington had lived, at the time, with her husband and three children at Blakeley, a mansion near Wheatlands, but the family were often guests of her sister and her husband's uncle at Mount Vernon. Bushrod Washington held Jane's husband as his favorite relative and intended him to inherit the famous estate. Jane and her family were there in 1826 when the Marquis de Lafayette came back, as an old man, to visit the Republic he had helped to form, and "Kitty," as Jane Washington called her foster-child, received a doll from the great Frenchman as he walked around the mansion, thinking of the days he had spent with General Washington.

That "Mamma Jane" spoiled little Kitty was the understanding of Kitty's descendants. "She tenderly loved and indulged her more than she did her own children, Maria, John Augustine, Jr., and Richard. . . . Kitty developed into a very attractive, wilful, red-headed child." [1]

When Kitty was nine, Uncle Bushrod Washington died, leaving Mount Vernon and its 4,000 acres to John Augustine, who with his family moved in, Kitty being assigned the room once occupied by Nellie Custis, step-daughter of George Washington. So favorably did the child take to the change that "she grew up provoked that she hadn't been born there." [2] Mount Vernon was "a mecca for every distinguished foreigner and a center of hospitality to the most cultured circles of American society. Once a year the President and Cabinet were entertained at dinner and the most distinguished statesmen and literary celebrities were frequent guests." [3] Kitty often saw Robert E. Lee, from nearby Arlington, and kin-folk added to the guest-list that grew and grew as Jane Washington and her husband expanded the proverbial hospitality of the national shrine.

(1) Mss. "Catherine Blackburn Turner" by her daughter, Maria Wright Ommanney.
   (2) Ibid.   (3) Ibid.

Each summer the family returned to the mountain air of Blakeley where Kitty saw her sister, Christina, who had remained with her father at Wheatlands.

This was not good for Kitty's already too-short temper, for it put her into touch with a step-mother whom she thought persecuted little 'Tina. Soon after her mother's death, Kitty's father had married the governess of the children, and Kitty thought she discriminated against 'Tina in favor of two daughters of her own. To Kitty, Sister 'Tina was in Cinderella's shoes, being dressed in "underclothes of unbleached cotton" while her step-sisters were dressed in finery. 'Tina told Kitty of the cruel whippings her step-mother gave her and how "her old black Mammy would frequently weep over the cuts, and anoint them with simple remedies." Once Kitty interfered when Mrs. Turner was whipping Christine, and pulling the high-backed comb out of the woman's hair "jabbed it into her head several times as hard as she could, then ran as fast as she could to Blakeley . . . and the shelter of Mrs. Washington's arms. She was compelled to apologize to her step-mother but she always detested her." [4]

Wit and mischief ran races in Kitty's mind. Once at least she climbed the portable steps beside a high curtained bed and dumped pitchers of cold water into the billowing feather-ticks so that her governess would be surprised that night, and at another time she leaned over the banister in the hall and jerked off the governess' wig with a fish-hook.

In 1832, only three years after taking over Mount Vernon, John Augustine died, leaving the property to his four-year-old son, and name-sake, with the boy's mother to manage it till he was twenty-one.

Although, with all the necessary entertaining, Jane Washington was hard put to it to make expenses, she sent

(4) Mss. "Catherine Blackburn Turner" and mss. "Reminiscences of My Life" by Maria Wright Ommanney.

Kitty to a Catholic convent at Emmettsburg, Maryland, where 'Tina also attended—a school keyed enough to the social demands of Virginia to cause the little girls to stand "in stocks with boards on their backs to give them a good carriage" and, for their complexions' sake to wear "masks over their faces when they rode horse-back."

As she grew up a social life of great charm came to Kitty, and as her own daughter, years later, heard it, "Hospitality was simply unbounded." Girls with "mulatto maids attending and slave coachman driving, "traveled in their own conveyances . . . staying over night or perhaps for weeks at a time at the beautiful plantation homes which extended from mountains to sea-level—Blakeley, Wheatlands, Rippon Lodge, Claymont, Smith's Mount, Brandon, Mount Airy, Kinlock."

Kitty always remembered that slavery was mainly a matter of "tender hereditary bonds uniting master and servant," and she liked to tell how the Mount Vernon butler stood outside the open dining room window, one day when she was entertaining a young clergyman from Alexandria, and remarked in perfectly audible tones, 'If I couldn't have no better beau dan a po' country parson, I wouldn't have no beau 'tall'." And how, after watching her show her high spirit and independence with so many suitors, another old butler at Mount Vernon warned her, "You'll walk through the cane brake and pick up a crooked stick at last, Miss Kitty."

Mrs. Washington, taking great pride in Kitty's dash, red hair, blue eyes, fine figure and wit, had trained her to sing and to play both the piano and guitar. To have her marry well was "Mamma Jane's" wish and, in the opinion of Kitty's daughter, the young woman was "so indulged all her life that in her the imperious Turner temper too often found expression."

Religious and perhaps Puritanic, Mrs. Washington was

dismayed to find that when Kitty did fall in love, it should
be with a Southern gentleman, officer in the United States
Army, who had a pronounced weakness for hard liquor.
Mamma Jane refused to permit the marriage unless the
suitor could demonstrate, by one year's total abstinence,
that his weakness was not permanent. But, according to
the story Kitty's children would hear, "the suitor held
out until the night before his year was up, but on that
night another Southern lady gave him a drink and he fell
by the wayside. Mrs. Washington forbade the marriage,
and Kitty was broken-hearted." That Kitty would love
the memory of this lost suitor all the rest of her life and
never give herself in complete romanticism to the man she
finally did marry, was the opinion of Kitty's daughter
in maturity.

Not long after the tragedy, Kitty was introduced to
John S. Wright, whom Mrs. Washington understood to
be "a wealthy Westerner visiting Washington on public
business" and when Wright laid suit to Kitty, Mamma
Jane urged her to accept. "Mrs. Washington was delighted
with the energetic young Westerner who was also a deeply
religious man in marked contrast to the train of suitors
who had wooed the brilliant and capricious belle who was
with difficulty, persuaded to put her head under the matri-
monial yoke." (5)

In Mrs. Washington's eyes it was time Kitty married;
she was twenty-six and there would be little wealth coming
to her or anybody else from Mount Vernon and its acres.
Guests, bearing letters of introduction from important
personages in the United States and Europe, were eating
Mrs. Washington out of house and home. She and her son,
John Augustine, were forced to devote almost their whole
time to the hospitable entertainment of persons who were
merely curious about George Washington, and, three years

(5) Ibid.

Mrs. John S. Wright (Kitty Turner)

after Kitty, as a bride, had moved away, young John Augustine, succeeding to the ownership, found himself near bankruptcy. He was forced to beg the United States government to help share the responsibility. Despite the obvious fairness of this petition, nothing would be done until February, 1860, when the Mount Vernon Ladies Association took over the house, tomb and 200 of the acres.[6]

So reluctant was Kitty to leave Mount Vernon that "she made him (Wright) promise to let her come back to Virginia every year." He agreed, and she did.

On September 1, 1846, the wedding took place at Blakeley. Her wedding veil and the lace which trimmed her dress were brought from Brussels. But according to family tradition, on the day of her wedding her former suitor, the army officer, shot himself.

The groom's mother and brother Timothy went on from Chicago for the wedding and Timothy liked to tell, in later years, "with what trepidation he, a raw Western youth, entered the most refined circles of American society, but he was so cordially made welcome that he soon lost all feeling of embarrassment."[7]

Kitty's first impression of Chicago was a bad one. Some of the alert Abolitionists of the city advised her Negro maid, Mollie, as they arrived, that she was free, now that she had been brought to Illinois. The slave girl, terrified at the prospect, gasped "I b'longs to Miss Kitty; that's who I b'longs to" and stood repeating it until her mistress rescued her.

From the stage, or carriage, Kitty was carried, across the deep mud, to the hotel and it affronted her to have "a brawny Irishman" do the carrying in place of the Negro coachmen who had always done such duties. As her daughter, Maria, described it, "John S. Wright had a comfort-

(6) "Mount Vernon, Its Owner and Its Story" by Harrison Howell Dodge.
(7) Mss. "Catherine Blackburn Turner" by Maria Wright Ommanney.

able home on Washington Street ready for his bride, but western society was so crude to the gently nurtured girl that she always detested Chicago, although she reigned there as a queen of society and entertained as no one else knew how to entertain. She always had a staff of servants, a boy trained to wait at table, a house-maid, laundress and nurse." Much chagrined to discover her mother-in-law, Huldah Dewey Wright, ironing her own caps, even after Kitty had explained they could be done by the servant "who did nothing but fine laundry work," Kitty had her Negro maid "secretly smuggle an iron into Mrs. Wright's bed-chamber" since she "was very solicitous lest the servants should think she was marrying into an inferior family, and she instructed her husband to be very liberal in his gifts."

Mechanization of prairie life—wind power and steam power. From *The Prairie Farmer*, June 30, 1859.

CHAPTER IX

Railroad Rhapsodies

THREE weeks after his wedding Wright was in Chicago, serving as head of the civic committee to welcome on October 8, 1846, the General State Educational Convention for which he had been drumming steadily in his paper. Before leaving for Virginia he had printed in his September issue an invitation for all delegates and teachers to stay in the homes of Chicagoans during the meeting, and in that same issue he had announced that a Teachers' Institute would be held for a week following the convention—inaugurating this new Eastern institution in the West.

Horace Mann had told him that he had found these institutes "more powerful in awakening a general interest in education than any other means yet discovered," and Wright had urged friends of education, across the State, to send their local teachers to the institute in Chicago— "Let one lend his wagon, another a span of horses, another a load of wheat which the teacher could take to market. . . . We consider the institute quite as important as the convention, itself."

As temporary secretary, program manager and, upon several occasions, speaker, at the convention, Wright found that his common school crusade was winning the support of prominent citizens in ever increasing numbers. He was exuberant at the success of the Teachers' Institute which ran for a full week after the Convention had adjourned, and which was addressed by notable Eastern

107

educators whom he imported. When the institute was copied across the West in succeeding months, he rejoiced —it would build sentiment for the Normal School, that fondest of his educational dreams.

The world was going his way. During the Convention the enthusiasm for schools grew to such proportions that a Northwestern Educational Society, embracing many States, was organized, also the Illinois Auxiliary of the newly created Board for National Education—and as everybody expected, Wright was secretary and general promoter of both.

With his mother's youthful example before him, and with her voice in his ear, Wright began to drive harder and harder for the employment of women teachers in the common schools. The conventions which he attended began regularly resolving in favor of the step, and Wright's paper devoted columns to the efforts of Henry Ward Beecher's sister, Catherine, to colonize New England's surplus of "school-ma'ams" on the Western frontier. Since women outnumbered the men in the East as much as men outnumbered the women in the West, a great guffaw had risen in the newspapers at this desire of "the old-maids of New England to get themselves a man."

Defending the project as a serious and important contribution, Wright in his July, 1847, issue, published Miss Beecher's description of fifty women whom she was preparing for their missionary venture into the wilds—"most are mature and experienced teachers and all but three are considerably over twenty. . . . All of them will be qualified to cut and fit dresses, and will bring with them the best patterns, not only for all their underclothing, but for children's garments. They will also know how to make the best kind of bread and yeast and to render themselves useful in various ways in any family with which they may be thrown . . . they would be willing to aid in doing their own washing and ironing and also aid in sweeping, making beds and such kinds of work as would give them healthful exercise and not interfere with their school duties."

A year later Wright began campaigning for higher salaries for both male and female teachers, pointing out that the nation paid each of its naval officers over $1,900 a year while the states paid school teachers on the following basis: Maine, $15.40 per month to males, $4.80 to females; New Hampshire, $13.50 to males, $5.65 to females; Connecticut, $16 and $6.50; New York, $14.96 and $6.69; Pennsylvania, $17.02 and $10.09; Ohio, $15.42 and $8.73; Indiana, $12 and $6; Michigan, $12.71 and $5.36. Even Massachusetts, which prided itself upon leading in education, paid only $8.07 to women, while giving men $24.51.

Illinois, by paying $18 and $10, stood even with Pennsylvania as a banner state in the treatment of women teachers. In '48 Illinois had 1,565 male and 966 female teachers, not one-half the number of qualified instructors necessary to supply even the scant 4,500 schoolhouses in the State. The State's school buildings themselves were still "miserably poor" in official words, and "there are 255,800 children without any schools" at all.

A year after Miss Beecher had sent out 110 New England "schoolma'ams" a check showed that 93 were still teaching and of those who had resigned, three were planning to return.

Often as he had written and spoken about the deficiencies in education in the West, Wright's passionate love of Chicago stirred him to scornful denial when, in 1847, a report issued from Springfield stated that Cook county only paid its teachers an average of $12 per month, ninety cents below the average for the State, and that of its 155,715 population under twenty years of age, only 46,814 attended school for any portion of the year.

Wright declared in reply that "in the city the three male teachers are paid $500 per annum, and the ten females from $200 to $250 each," while the schools in the rural portions of the county could not bring down the average to $12. Also, he insisted, more than one-third of the children did attend school.

He had worked tirelessly for the betterment of schools in his home town and had been one of the leaders in persuading its citizens to tax themselves for the support of education. Up to 1843, as he reviewed the story in his April, 1847, number, the city rented two old houses, one story in height, frail and flimsy, and set flush with the street on two sides, while a third was owned outright by the city. One teacher in each tried to manage, respectively, 85, 97 and 115 youngsters. The rented buildings were obtained at $60 a month, and "when it is remembered," Wright said, "that buildings in this city rent for from 20 to 40 per cent of their value, some idea of this seminary of learning may be formed." The schoolhouse belonging to the city, in 1844, crowded 142 pupils into a room not large enough for half that number, yet had to turn away applicants for admission. That year the city sold it, receiving, even on a rising real estate market, only $60.

"In 1844 the city had reached a crisis in its school matters," said Wright. Wisely it chose to build large houses, "and though this met with strong opposition and the most fearful predictions were made concerning it, we believe that its wisdom is generally, if not universally, at present, concurred with." The first, an experimental building, was made of brick. An innovation—an $800 furnace—was installed in this building, but "has since been abandoned as the expense was so enhanced that it well-nigh upset the whole system." In the summer of 1845 another house was built on the north side of the river, at a cost of some $4,000 and, in the summer of 1846, a third, costing around $5,000, was erected. All three were of brick, two stories in height and were financed by a property tax.

In July, 1849, Wright estimated that the city held some 8,000 children of school age and, of these, 2,000 were in public school the whole term, while almost 2,000 were in the twenty private schools that had been established. Many Chicagoans considered "public schools too plebian. ... Others wish a decidedly religious training," factors that held back, in his view, the public schools. A fourth public building was soon to be built, but all four were merely "primary and nothing more. Higher places of education are not yet provided. To meet the wants of such, our private schools are established."

It worried him that Chicago's foreign born—one-third of its total population in 1849—"can't be induced to educate their children. . . . The multitudes coming from the lanes and hovels of the city must have a place of instruction afforded them." The population increased more rapidly than the school facilities.

The arrival of children in his own household was stirring him to take more active interest in the particular schools of his city. The first, Augustine Washington, had been born on May 29, 1847. The second, Walter, named for his bachelor uncle, had died a few months after his birth in September, 1848, and a third, a girl named Maria Alexander had arrived on October 19, 1849. The fourth and final child, Chester Dewey, would be born July 5, 1852.

It was the recollection of Maria, in after years, that all her brothers, like herself, had been born at Blakeley, back in Virginia, so ardently did her mother hate Chicago and hold her husband to his prenuptial promise that she be allowed to revisit her old home at least once a year. For some and perhaps all of these births, Wright accompanied his wife to her old home, but he was back in Chicago soon after the birth of his first son to take part in the famous

Rivers and Harbors Convention which on July 5, 1847, drew to Chicago statesmen, editors, notables from all over the North.

This event, signalling as it did the Northwest's demands for a share of Federal internal improvement money, was tremendously exciting to Wright. Here was a chance to convince Eastern visitors of the startling future railroads would bring the West. Mingling with the delegates and distinguished visitors he found that "he could name each State's representative in the procession as it passed by, as personal acquaintances."[1] And among them he found one particularly responsive soul, Joseph T. Buckingham, an influential politician and editor of the *Boston Courier*, a newspaper which, two years before, had published some letters Wright had sent it describing the glories of Western prospects.

When he found Buckingham's "interest in public improvements not confined to the East," Wright established such relations as caused Buckingham to announce in his paper on August 27 the start of a series of Wright's articles on Western Railroads "which will be of much interest to the business men and capitalists of Boston."

The first articles which Wright penned before leaving for Virginia to see his wife and baby, pointed out to Eastern investors the wisdom of helping finance the railroad which Chicago was proposing to build to Galena. Only seventeen days earlier, the subscription books had been opened in Galena, Chicago and the towns between. Wright warned the Easteners what would happen unless the road northwestward to the Mississippi River were built: another would start from St. Louis and, running through Terre Haute and Indianapolis, would reach Cincinnati and thus carry Western trade to Baltimore and Philadelphia, those hated rivals of Boston and New York.

(1) In Memoriam: John S. Wright, by Augustine W. Wright.

"But," said Wright, "let the best channels of intercom-
munication be so arranged as to direct travel from the
West and Southwest by way of the Lakes to Buffalo . . .
and the merchant is then almost as likely to go to Boston
. . . and the New England city is placed beyond rivalry
with Philadelphia, Baltimore and other Southern cities."

The Rivers and Harbors Convention had started a campaign which would end, Wright predicted, with Federal
improvements of the Mississippi so that the rich trade of
the lower river would come up to Galena and transfer
cargoes to the proposed railroad. This road, offering such
limitless trade to the East, could only be built with capital
from Boston and New York. "We have not enough capital
to spare in the West and of the $2,700,000 which the road
will cost, not over $500,000 can be depended upon from
Chicago and Galena and intermediate points."(2)

In a second article, written from the steamboat Louis-
ana which took him by the lakes route to Buffalo, the
Western editor warned Boston and New York that within
a few years a railroad from Pittsburgh would divert the
Ohio steamboat cargoes directly to Philadelphia and Baltimore. Next would come a railroad from Pittsburgh
through Columbus, Ohio, to St. Louis, and both Boston
and New York would become merely "tributary, or at
least secondary, to their Southern rivals."(3)

The Eastern cities, he went on, could not "be assured
that the legislature of Illinois would always do them as
much good service as was rendered last winter, in refusing
to charter a company to conduct a railroad from St. Louis
to Terre Haute." Illinois, for selfish reasons, would prefer
to build up cities "within its own borders and to send the
trade and travel through its length, rather than across it"
but "Illinois cannot long act the dog in the manger." Un-

(2) *Boston Courier,* August 27, 1847.
(3) *Boston Courier,* September 23, 1847.

less the Galena and Chicago was speedily financed, other interests would provide the money for a road which would send Western trade across to Baltimore.

By the end of 1848 the Michigan Railroad would be as far east as New Buffalo, Michigan, and might reach Chicago by 1849. The New York and Erie Railroad was rushing toward completion. Boston could protect itself against losing trade to New York by financing the Galena and Chicago so that it could be ready when the Michigan line got into town. "Subscribe liberally" was his refrain; dividends would be large; the stake was control of vast Western riches to come.

Frankly, in his letters to newspapers, and in the series of circulars on railroads and Western real estate opportunities which came flying from his presses, he confessed that he expected to make money through Chicago's growth. He prophesied his own prosperity, and begged all who had faith to join him in his march to glory. But above and beyond his self-interest there was beginning to glow, in his writings, a belief for and love of Chicago that verged on the mystic. There was ecstacy in his vision of the city. It was the Promised Land.

Never, in later years, did he write with bitterness of the ridicule or at best, the tolerant incredulity with which influential Chicagoans met his hosannahs to Chicago's future. Even his friend William B. Ogden, president of the Galena and Chicago, pooh-poohed some of Wright's rhapsodic forecasts of what that road would do for Chicago. Wright recalled how "one of these millionaires, when efforts were made to start the Galena railroad, argued against it, because railroads would stop the advent of the prairie schooners, 50 to 1,500 of them daily arriving, and with the stoppage 'grass would grow in the streets' was his sagacious declaration."

Even when Wright in 1848 threw himself into the fight

to create the Illinois Central Railroad as the line which would give Illinois the wished-for passage from end to end of the State—connecting Chicago with Cairo—a rich reactionary in Chicago said to Wright, "Why, don't you see that the roads will enable farmers to run off their produce to Cairo while the river and canal are frozen, which, if kept to spring, would have come to Chicago?"

Wright answered, "Don't you see that that gives the farmers of central Illinois the advantage over others in the choice of markets? Whatever the course of the carrying trade, you may risk the prosperity of Chicago upon its popularity with the farmers."

It did not help Wright's reputation as a prophet without honor in his own city when, in the spring of 1848, he paid Bronson $45,000 for a second block. Wright admitted the sum was "at least double what it was worth" at the time, but the future would make it a bargain, indeed. "Though so clear to me," he afterward said, "there was not a man in Chicago, to my knowledge, with whom Mr. Bronson could have made the contracts." Some of the shrewdest real estate dealers in town sold lots next his new purchase that winter at a rate considerably less than half the price he had paid—and counted themselves lucky. Sixteen years later the rents from the two Bronson blocks had enabled Wright to pay out $147,000 on principal, interest, taxes, etc., and were valued in land alone at over $400,000. The astute sharpers who had sold one of the neighboring lots so wisely—getting $4,500 for it—saw its price go to $80,000 in the same length of time.

In 1846 Wright had coveted "the best lot on the north side, 80 feet on the river and North Water street and 189 feet on Clark (a bridge) street" which was offered at $6,000. For years he urged friends to buy it but it was not until 1850 that he coaxed two Virginia friends to take it at $9,000. Six years later it was valued at $110,000 and had given them "a good ground rent" each year.

He knew that it was short-sighted for one of his brothers, in the spring of 1850, to insist upon release as a guarantor of the notes on the second Bronson block. Its future was so plain, but the brother needed money, and "he had acted generously toward me—few brothers would have done as much—and his request was reasonable, nothwithstanding it involved such a sacrifice of my expectations. The block, first bought for $37,500, was sold for $60,000 to the Galena Railroad for a depot. It saddened him that nobody would lend him the money with which he could have paid off the debt and have freed his brother without selling the land. "I could not make capitalists see through my spectacles," he said.

However, two of the lots in the second Bronson block, "equal in value to about one-fourth of the purchase," which would have made them cost $1,125 all told, soon were bringing him $7,000 a year in rent, with "the lessee paying all taxes and assessments."

And by 1856, in the words of his son, Augustine, "his real estate was valued at over $600,000, a great fortune for those days." But it was always Wright's fate to be predicting so many new glories by the time sober fact had proved his earlier prophecies correct, that those who had laughed at him originally forgot to recognize their error. Always ahead of the staid, conservative business men in his vision, his excitable manner and rush of fresh predictions prevented them from recognizing his essential soundness as to real estate values.

His beliefs scouted by his fellow-townsmen, his wife and frequently by his brothers, he found intense pleasure in the company of his children. Maria delighted to tell how "every morning he gathered his three little children around him for family prayers, reading from the Bible and commending us for the day to the watchful care of

our Heavenly Father." He wrote them long, often and
tenderly while away on business, and kept them amused
with dogs, rabbits, swings, a carriage, a sleigh, a black
pony. Having in 1851 as he said, rentals coming in to the
tune of "several thousand dollars above annual payments,"
he had the celebrated artist G. P. A. Healy paint his wife
and children, and was proud of Kitty as "in a dark green
habit and a hat with white plumes" she rode the horse he
had bought for her, "a very beautiful Arabian whose skin
shone like silver." Once his family returning from Virginia found that "as a surprise to his wife" he had added
another story to their home on Washington Street opposite the future site of Marshall Field and Company. Of
the home life, Maria wrote in later years:

"My mother thought seven servants the least number
necessary for her household, and said she kept an Irish
boarding-house, but they were a warm-hearted lot and she
must have been a very kind mistress. . . . She entertained
as no one else in Chicago knew how to entertain, but she
was actually insulted when an account of one of her dinner
parties was published in the paper. . . . We always lived
so that guests were welcome, but one day when my father
unexpectedly brought two gentlemen home to dinner, my
mother called a caterer to serve the repast, so, probably,
he did not offend again. . . . Wine was always on our table
and even we children had wine and water and sugar, but
I don't believe my father ever drank enough to affect him."

Maria grew up understanding that her father had done
something very generous for his wife's aunt, Mrs. Jane
Washington, when she had, around 1850, freed such of her
slaves as would migrate to Liberia. He had "given her
$40,000 with which to equip a ship." And, sitting in her
father's pew in the Second Presbyterian Church, Maria
liked to think how he had given the stone for the building
from a quarry he owned. Wright and his mother had been

among the twenty-six Chicagoans who had in 1842 started this Second Presbyterian—a $1,600 shanty on Randolph, a little east of Clark—and they had been in the forefront of the work when it had been abandoned for a new church, a $40,000 building at Washington and Wabash.

It would be this church that would stand out in the mind of William Bross, the Chicago newspaper publisher, as a fine example of Wright's foresight of Chicago's future: "When the Second Presbyterian Church was finished in 1850, then by far the best church edifice in the city, a number of gentlemen were discussing its substantial and other characteristics, when some one remarked that 'it would stand a thousand years.'

" 'Nonsense,' said Mr. Wright, 'it will not be fifty years before it will have to be moved to make way for business.' It stood on the corner of Wabash avenue and Washington street, far removed from the business portions of Lake and Water streets. Before twenty years had elapsed it was, indeed, in the way of business. Mr. Wright had thirty years to spare in his prediction."

As early as 1847 or '48, Wright proposed that Chicago buy land on its outskirts "for a large park in each division and connected by a wide avenue, to be extended along the lake shore at the north and south, surrounding the City with avenues and parks."(4) But his argument that the land would later cost fantastically more went unheeded.

In the October, 1853, issue of *The Prairie Farmer*, Wright's horticultural editor, Dr. John A. Kennicott criticised "the oversight in not providing sufficient public grounds in the original plans of our Western cities" and pointed out that Chicago, which had nicknamed itself "The Garden City" still had time—"to secure grounds for parks and gardens somewhat worthy of her heroic appellation and prospective population." He urged that the city buy

(4) Chicago: Past, Present, Future, by John S. Wright.

some 300 acres of woodland around "Pine Grove on the lake shore, some three miles from Lake street" from the two pieces of wild, cheap lands owned, respectively, by James H. Rees and John S. Wright. It would be 1859 before the city organized its south, west and north park commissions and installed, at a staggeringly higher cost, the system which Wright had urged in the modest days of 1847.

When he had reached manhood, Chester Wright, the youngest of Wright's children, liked to think back upon the days when his father "would stimulate my thought by starting me on something properly, and I well remember his delight when I worked it out. I most often see him as he appeared at Lake Forest when I had a recitation at commencement exercises. His head was held high, his whole mind centered on me. I could fairly feel the pride he had in me."

That Wright's three children should have attended private schools, the boys at Lake Forest, and Maria at Dearborn Seminary in Chicago, then at Miss Howland's in the East and finally Vassar, was to be interpreted as another of his concessions to his wife's demands. It was highly probable that she included his passion for common schools in her general indictment of his "visionary ideas," and it was obvious that her own love for and pride in her children made it seem imperative that they should have a schooling as near as possible to the fashionable upbringing she considered herself to have had.

CHAPTER X

No Land Monopoly

"**P**ERHAPS it may be thought extravagant to insist that John S. Wright did more than any one man to build the Illinois Central Railway, and therefore to aid in the development of our vast railway system," wrote William Bross, one of the editors of the *Chicago Tribune*, when he reviewed historic days.(¹)

He thought is not extravagant at all, but would set down the facts and let the reader judge for himself.

Since the early 1830s Wright heard vague talk about the Cairo Company's attempt to build a railroad from the southern tip of Illinois to Galena. The plan had never gotten anywhere until one of the State's Senators in Washington, Sidney Breese, began in the late 1840s, to plead with Congress to finance the road. Even then, public sentiment had been lacking. Farmers feared the trains would frighten their cows, and business men feared that the State, still teetering on the brink of bankruptcy, would utterly collapse under the burden of the taxation which the road would occasion.

In 1848, however, Breese had been joined in Washington by Illinois' junior Senator, Stephen A. Douglas, who decided to sponsor national legislation granting Western lands to the railroad. As a friend of Wright's who had recently moved to Chicago where he had heavy real estate investments, Douglas saw eye to eye with the farm editor on many things. Douglas was a Democrat and Wright

(1) *Chicago Tribune,* September 30, 1874.

120

was enough of a Whig, in spite of his heresies on the high tariff, to make attempts, however unsuccessful, to get himself appointed postmaster in Chicago after his party had won the presidential election in the autumn of 1848.

Intensely interested in Western railroads, as he was, Wright fairly burst into ecstacy when he discovered that Douglas was changing his proposed legislation so that the railroad would come to Chicago as well as to Galena, tapping the most populous parts of Northern Illinois.

Here was the thing that would tie together in an irresistible forward surge, the two objects of his dreaming passion—Chicago and the prairies. Wright seized his pen and poured his ideas, his arguments into a pamphlet or "circular" as he called it, urging Westerners to digest the assembled facts and then mail their approval to Senator Douglas in Washington.

As he wrote, his imagination soared higher and higher, and he wrote another circular addressing further arguments to Southerners; then a third, aimed at Easterners. A full 6,000 copies in all were printed and posted at his own expense, each bearing a petition which citizens could sign and forward to their representatives in Congress praying support of Douglas' bill.

William Bross, who was close to Wright at the time in Chicago, saw that "Mr. Wright forwarded (the circulars) to every postmaster between the Lake and the Gulf. For weeks and months these petitions came pouring into Congress by the hundreds and, taking advantage of this overwhelming expression of public opinion, our Senators and Representatives produced the passage of the bill. . . . Mr. Wright kept the spare time of his clerk occupied for weeks in sending off the petitions . . . he furnished the influence by which the grant was obtained."[2]

Wright, himself, never went so far in claiming credit

(2) Ibid.

for the passage of the land grant bill. He merely said that "Judge Douglas said they (the circulars) came to Washington by the hundreds, numerously signed and had much influence, being the earliest movement for this object outside of Congress, except by the Cairo Company."[3] Wright would say, in later years, however, that his efforts for the grant had been, in the beginning "regarded as a wild goose chase . . . one of those visionary schemes resulting in such practical benefits that for one I am proud to have had a hand in its accomplishment."[4]

There were, in time, Illinois newspapers to push the cause, but Wright had been the first to stir up national interest and had done it with the device he had used so effectively in Illinois school reform—the circular with petition attached. What Bross failed to mention in his great tribute to Wright was the emphasis the circulars put upon the long North-South railroad as a force that would unify the States in a time when the aftermath of the Mexican War had precipitated slavery into the vortex of sectional hate.

Bitter debates were taking form in Congress, but Wright in his circular to the South was promising that if that section would sign petitions for the Illinois Central Railroad, he and his friends in Illinois would work for a similar grant to the road that was projected from Mobile to Cairo. Build both roads, said he, and a Southerner can come to Cairo and be within three and a half days of New York. The South and the West should merge their interests. As things stood, Southern produce was stopped by the Ohio River's ice all winter long, while, with the Mississippi always open as far north as Cairo, the new railroad "would give uninterrupted communication between the extremes of the Union at all times of the year."

To New York and Boston his circular pointed out how

(3) Chicago: Past, Present and Future, by John S. Wright, 1870. P. 22.
(4) Ibid.

much greater a control of Western and Southern trade
would come through the Illinois Central than through
the Galena and Chicago of which he had previously told
them. In 1848 he also sent a series of letters to the *Boston
Mining Journal and Railroad Gazette* and to the *New
York Courier and Enquirer,* insisting that railroads would
be the "iron bands by which States separated by thousands
of miles, are to be bound together in indissoluble union.
As each link is added to this great chain, the patriot and
philanthropist must rejoice . . ."

When the land grant bill came up in Congress, it called
for a road that would sweep from Chicago clear to Mobile,
via Cairo, and gave huge totals to three states, Illinois'
share being 2,595,000 acres. With Senator Douglas smooth-
ing the way, the Senate passed the bill on May 3, 1850, by
a vote of 26 to 14, but in the House of Representatives
there was stiffer opposition and, late in August, Wright
went to Washington to help lobby it through. For three
weeks he worked among the Congressmen, and "as a son
of the Bay State and a Whig" spent much time with the
members of the Massachusetts delegation.

It angered him to find some of them agreeing that the
land grant was right, but refusing to vote for it because
the agricultural West wouldn't share the high protective
tariff views of the East. To one, a clergyman in private
life, who admitted such reasoning, Wright broke out with,
"You're a pretty Representative of Massachusetts. A man
of your cloth to violate your oath, and vote against a bill
you admit is every way desirable and just, because Western men will not violate their oaths and favor protection
which they conscientiously believe to be wrong."(5)

The passage of the bill, donating alternate sections for
six miles on each side of the road to finance construction,
came on September 20, 1850, as a great victory, but to

(5) Ibid.

Wright it meant only the beginning of another fight—the
fight to force the Illinois Legislature to protect the public
in its chartering of the railroad. In *The Prairie Farmer*,
and in letters to the *Chicago Journal*, and in a circular
which he wrote and broadcast, he demanded that the new
road pay handsomely into the State treasury. "The grants
can be squandered," he said in the November, 1850,
Prairie Farmer, "and made to the State an evil instead
of a benefit. . . . We trust the eyes of the people will be
upon their legislators, and let them know and understand
that by no scheme of villainy and corruption, however
hidden, will they be allowed to shirk from responsibility."

There were those, he said in his circular, who favored
surrendering the lands to a company on condition that the
State debt he paid, but that the road's responsibility should
stop there. "They have so little confidence in public man-
agement, both now and in the future, that they would
voluntarily throw away a large and perpetual income for
fear that it would be misused, and become a source of
bribery and corruption . . . for one, I have no sympathy
with the forlorn and traducing sentiment which would
deprive the State of vast wealth for fear of its abuse."

Another plan, advanced by James Wadsworth, financial
agent for the State, would have the holders of Illinois'
depreciated bonds build the road, operate it until they had
their money safely out. Then when the railroad obliga-
tions had been paid off, too, the Illinois Central would
revert to the State.

Wright, himself, was for the Wadsworth plan except
that when all indebtedness, State and road, had been paid,
the company should own and operate the line, give the
State a "just proportion" of its net income. The great
issue was the extinction of the State debt; and unless the
Legislature brought this happy consummation out of the
situation, "Illinois will be everlastingly dishonored."

Into the fight, Wright projected another grant of land which Congress on September 28, 1850, had bestowed upon the States—millions of acres of swamp lands lying on what was called "The American Bottom." Douglas had told Wright that Illinois' share would amount to some 1,800,000 acres, and Wright in his circular urged that this be used in building other railroads and kept as stock in the lines "which will pay from 10 to 20 per cent dividends." These dividends should pay the debt of that ancient School, College and Seminary Fund which he had been trying to rescue for twelve years. Where in his early researches he had discovered these taxes to have been "borrowed" he, now, in his circular charged flatly that they had been "stolen", leaving the schools to be supported by direct tax. "No object compares in importance with that of educating the people . . . and the best disposition to make of any surplus from them (the Swamp Lands) is to add it to the school fund."

Pounding at this, the newest approach to his pet crusade, Wright won, the Legislature on June 22, 1852, giving the lands—1,457,399 acres—to the several counties "for purposes of education . . . or construction of roads and bridges or to such other purposes." Most of it in time went to the schools.(6)

But forces too powerful to overthrow defeated Wright's plan for the railroad land grant. A group of Eastern promoters and capitalists—the Neal-Griswold organization—either with logic, advertising, retainer fees, sound business arguments or bribery, won over so many powerful politicians and newspaper editors that they cried down Wadsworth and Wright and, amid charges of corruption in the Legislature, got the coveted charter. They enlisted much support by charging that if the State bondholders built the road, control would be in the hands of scattered

(6) The Illinois Central Railroad; Paul Wallace Gates, pp. 101-102.

Easterners and foreigners, and would constitute a "monopoly."

Wright fought on to salvage what he could from the wreck, and as his son Augustine later described it: when "the legislature decided to transfer the land-grant to a corporation" he began a public drive insisting "that in return the said corporation should, during the continuance of its existence, pay ten per cent of its gross earning from operation to the State in lieu of other taxes. The legislature in its wisdom reduced this payment to seven per cent. After the bill had passed the president of the Illinois-Central Railroad told him they *would* have paid the ten per cent rather than relinquish the project. These payments had amounted to $9,833,258.61, Oct. 31, 1884, and paid the State debt. So far as I know, no other State possesses a like revenue, and Illinois owes these millions chiefly to the efforts of John S. Wright."[7]

Although Wright's efforts had been influential, it was the opinion of later researchers that a certain per cent of the road's earnings would have been given the State even without the pressure of Wright's campaign. Senator Douglas had come out for the issuing of the charter to the Neal-Griswold group, and it might well have ruined his political fortunes if the road had not promised a fair percentage to the State.

Wright's vigilance did not halt with the award of the land grants to the corporation. Studying the company's operations as the work progressed, he became convinced that one group of its directors were preparing to keep a large part of the granted lands away from public sale so that the price would increase. The expectation had been that the company would sell off these lands to actual settlers; now he saw the very "monopoly" which had been vaguely charged against his plan actually developing on

(7) In Memoriam: John S. Wright, by Augustine W. Wright.

the prairie. He had met monopoly before when speculators withheld timber from farmers who desperately needed fence rails, and here it was again—in farm land.

While in Washington, early in 1852 he studied the bills which, now that the government had committed itself to subsidizing railroads, were pouring out acreage to other lines. He asked his friends in the United States Senate and House what was being done in these new acts to prevent such favored speculation in land as the Illinois Central was now exhibiting. The reply was disappointing; the passage of safeguarding clauses was doubtful.

Home he came in April to make his May *Prairie Farmer* ring with the demand that his readers "write directly to any members of Congress whom they know, and to influential persons elsewhere, and enlist all the support possible," for these safeguards. He published the resolutions of Illinois mass-meetings condemning the Illinois Central land monopoly and urging Congress, "for the protection of the industrial classes," to check the speculators.

He told his readers the evil had been done, "The Company have the power to do as they will with their lands, irrespective of the rights and the interests of individuals and the public." Some of the railroad's directors had the right attitude, and wanted to sell the lands as rapidly as possible to bona fide settlers "at moderate prices," but others were plotting to hold large portions till the price had climbed. Unless the speculators were forced to disgorge "the State will be made to feel the heaviest weight of land monopoly ever known in this country," and "is destined to groan heavily for years and years."

Wright's daughter, Maria, remembered vaguely in later years that her father had gone to England "at his own expense and negotiated the bonds" for the Illinois Central. Since the promoter of that road, David Neal, had been in London in May, 1852, obtaining a loan of $5,000,000 from a British syndicate, it was not likely that Wright's visit, in October of that year, was for the same purpose.

It was possible that in his excitement over "the land monopoly" he did try to speed up foreign purchases of bonds so that the road could have sufficient working capital to allow it to sell the lands cheaply and on easy terms to settlers. But it was far more probable that he had gone to London to try and arrange for the export of American wool to English mills, since he was, at the time, financially interested in forcing the New England mills to pay Western wool producers higher prices. Also it was equally probable that he had sailed abroad in imitation of Cyrus McCormick and Obed Hussey who, like himself were manufacturing reapers and both of whom had gained international publicity for their patented machines by exhibiting them at the Great Exhibition in London during the summer of 1851. There was to be another International Exhibition opening at Dublin in May, 1853, and reapers were to be displayed there in force.

Whatever it was that took Wright to England, he was home in April, 1853, telling his readers that the visit had served "only to satisfy one more and more with this our own blest land."

Busy though he was with changes in the staff of his paper and with the promotion of his reaper and wool commission business, he kept a watchful eye on the railroad's "land monopoly." He warned the Legislators in January, 1854, that they had better have "a sharper eye for the interests of the State than of the Company" and that some of them had better "move an amendment requiring annual sale of the lands under a suitable appraisal." In Springfield he lobbied for an amendment to the Company's charter which would oblige the road to sell large areas annually "at a minimum appraisal to actual settlers." The speculators inside the Company's directorate must be whipped. He saw the amendment come to vote—and win by one "Yea." Then came the sudden and sickening climax! Representative Enos of Sangamon county changed his vote, and the amendment was lost!

Wright returned to the fight, blasting the "evil" again in his June, 1854, issue. In the words of one historian of the Illinois Central, "The persistent criticisms of this paper *(The Prairie Farmer)* did not cease until the Company inserted a large advertisement of its lands in the issue of February, 1855, when they finally ceased."[8]

The value of this implication that Wright was venial was to be weighed against the same historian's admission that in January and February, 1855, new officials of the railroad put through "necessary reforms," eliminating a clique of men who "were using their position as directors of the railroad to aid a land speculating venture." The reformers also reorganized the system of pricing acreage and undertook "at last a thorough examination of the land."[9]

Wright, himself, called attention to the advertisement in his February, 1855, issue, and cited it as proof that the Company was abandoning its practice of "monopoly." It was with the tone of a man who has won a long fight that he wrote down his pleasure at seeing how the advertisement "put these lands in market on such terms as will enable any man with health and a reasonable amount of energy, to pay for them almost or altogether entirely out of their own proceeds."

(8) The Illinois Central Railroad; Paul Wallace Gates, p. 152.
(9) Ibid. PP. 166-8.

CHAPTER XI

Wool Depots and Fried Food

AS Wright, entering his forties, reached the fullness of his powers, he was driven forward by two motives—to make money for himself and his family, and to serve and protect the public. He had spent time and money on the Illinois Central project because he wanted the road to come quickly and increase his real estate values in Chicago, but he had been willing to see the work delayed unless the public's interests were safeguarded.

For all his admiration of wealth as the legitimate patron of the West's development, he was catching glimpses of the danger for democracy that lay in the rising power of corporations. In the midst of his efforts to check the land-monopolistic wing of the Illinois Central directorate, he began to foster a Western revolt against the practices of the Eastern mills which dominated the wool market.

Just as he had been one of the earliest advocates of railroads for the West, he had been one of the first to urge prairie farmers to raise sheep; and in each case he found that when his goal had been reached there loomed ahead an even harder fight to keep the victory in the hands of the settlers.

In the late 1830s he had discovered that immigrants from the East still held a sectional notion that "the prairies were too level for sheep; affording no protection against winds, or chance for climbing, of which sheep are

130

WOOL

Received, Sorted and Sold at

WRIGHT'S WOOL DEPOT,

CHICAGO,

FOR ONE CENT AND A HALF PER POUND.

Interest charged on advances, and insurance at cost, say 30 to 40 cents on $100. No other expenses. Sacks paid for at their value.

Wool sold only for Cash or its Equivalent.

When a sale is made, the owner will be immediately notified, and payments made on demand, or remitted to order, less the cost of exchange. ☞ The consignor shall lways find either his wool or his money.

(From The Prairie Farmer, March, 1852.)

so fond; also that the open range was too hot in summer and too cold in winters. To this he answered in his paper that "the winds of the prairies are more stiff and steady than among the hills of New England, but are not so searching and terriffic. Chimneys are seldom blown down here, and we have never known a roof blown off although rafters are merely nailed down."

In his first years as editor and secretary of the Union Agricultural Society, he had kept preaching wool as a prairie crop, hunting out instances where it was successful and publishing the facts with satisfaction. "This is going to be a great country for growing wool" was his theme and he urged Eastern capitalists to lend prairie settlers money so that they each could buy from five to fifty sheep.

Even with the State's tax receipts hopelessly inadequate, he threw his paper's influence behind the plea of some farmers that the Legislature pass a law exempting sheep from taxation for a year so that poor men might make a start in wool-growing.

But late in 1843 he found that both the Western settlers and the Eastern newspapers had taken the pro-sheep propaganda too seriously, if anything; the talk was now that wool-growing was to be on a grandiose scale with vast herds feeding free on the open range.

In his October, 1843, issue appeared an editorial warning that such dreams were vain; "The lands are fast passing into the hands of private owners; and the time will soon be here when most of the land will belong to somebody." By September, 1844, *The Prairie Farmer* was saying "The rush of sheep to Illinois, Wisconsin, Iowa and Missouri is a perfect tornado. The demand is so great in Ohio that prices have risen 100 per cent in a few weeks."

Even with settlers, through ignorance and carelessness, losing hundreds of sheep by pushing them hard through

rains and fords on the drive from the Ohio sheep-growing
reservoirs to the prairies, the rush was sufficient to jump
Chicago's wool receipts from 1,500 pounds in '42 to 96,636
in '44 and to 246,610 in 1845. The last gain had been
achieved in spite of the death of thousands and thousands
of sheep in the bitter cold which swept the prairies in the
winter of 1844-45. In October, 1845, Wright's paper returned to its warnings against the romantic idea of free
grass:

"Allowing that every farmer in Illinois could have ac-
cess to the wild prairies, if he depended on nothing else his
sheep must die off, to the last one, twice in each year. The
grass on the wild prairie starts so as to afford feed for
sheep the first of June, and continues good feed for three
months, and affords some pasture for a month longer, unless a frost happens, in which case all are killed dead as
a herring. . . . A flock of sheep will completely ruin a piece
of wild grass in a very little time . . . gnaw it to the earth.

"But open prairie, desirable for pasture, is not accessi-
ble probably to one tenth of the farmers in this State. The
great majority live on land of their own purchase from
which the wild grass rapidly disappears. . . . The true way
to grow wool here, as elsewhere, is to purchase a farm,
stock down a good part of it to grass, and put another part
in cultivation for grain, roots, etc., and keep the flock at
home."

The paper lavished upon the farmers descriptions of
better breeds—especially the Merino; it printed veter-
inary suggestions, listing sometimes, for a solid page, medicines used in treating sheep diseases, and trumpeted the
glorious news when the 1848 figures showed that Chicago's shipments of wool by lake schooners to Buffalo had
gone past 960,500 pounds—and representing, at that, less
than half the State's estimated production. The average
clip, which had been three to three and one-half pounds

at the start of the '40s had gone up, nobody could say how much, although some thought to five.

That the prairies with all their land, all their streams for water-wheels, should be shipping their wool away and "paying vast sums annually for necessary clothing" from the East, worried Wright and his editor, Ambrose Wight, and in 1847 they gave prominence to the success of the weaving factories which had sprung up at Elgin and Joliet. But it was early in that year, in the January issue, that Wright began urging a more immediate measure of relief for the Western wool-growers—the establishment of a wool depot which would sort the clip and, selling direct to the agents of Eastern manufacturers, obtain much better prices for its clients. The idea had been launched three years before when the wool-growers of Duchess county, New York, pooling their clips and forcing buyers to make competitive bids, had received from 6 to 8 cents a pound more than their neighbors.

Noting this J. P. Blanchard, President of the Agricultural Society, announced at the next New York State Fair that the salvation of the wool-grower would be the establishment of permanent depots operated on a low commission basis. This the New York Society did at Kinderhook and at Buffalo Depot, and speedily the news passed among the wool producers, kindling enthusiasm especially in the minds of two sheep raisers and wool commission men, Perkins and Brown, who were operating near Akron, Ohio.

The junior partner, Brown, moved east in 1846 to open a depot at Springfield, Massachusetts, close to the big mills, while Perkins remained in Ohio near the greatest source of supply. For forty-one of his forty-six years John Brown had lived in Ohio as a farmer, tanner and shepherd, and was known as a contentious and religious man, ever alert to protect his rights, and forever suing or being sued over business deals.

Soon after setting up at Springfield, he wrote one of his customers, "We have at last found out that some of the principal manufacturers are leagued together to break us down." There was to be a national Wool-Growers Convention at Steubenville on February 10, 1847, and he hoped every wool producer in the country would be there "to hear statements about the wool trade of a most interesting character." One thing would correct the evils, he said; it was "to get the broad-shouldered, hard-handed farmers to understand how they have been imposed upon."

The meeting, whose proceedings John S. Wright enthusiastically read—and published—was as Brown had hoped, widely attended by delegates from Northwestern Virginia, Western Pennsylvania and Eastern Ohio. It was a letter from L. A. Morrell of Tompkins county, New York, which, as read to the convention, best summarized the national problem:

"To determine the real value of our wool, it is necessary to know accurately the cost of manufacturing the various styles and qualities, and the prices in market. This is a species of information manufacturers are quite too shrewd to impart, especially to the wool-grower. . . . That the really fine wools grown in the United States have been sold much below their true value for a number of years past, is . . . not susceptible of any doubt. This is proved by the large profits or dividends declared by a number of fine woolen manufactories, and among others, the Middlesex Company, which recently announced a dividend of 16 per cent for the last year . . . the manufacturers have treated us very badly."

He described the system whereby the small farmers took their fleeces to town in blankets and threw themselves "upon the tender mercies of one, two or more greedy speculators who often combine, or at all events buy only at very reduced prices. . . . The farmer, rather than return

home, sells it." Farmers who had larger clips "waited for
the coming of itinerant agents . . . a class of men very
probably designated 'wool sharks' . . . sent forth armed
with orders to buy as cheap as they can. . . . Their humbug
stories, to practice upon the credulous, are cut from the
whole cloth." A third method was to ship the wool direct
to the manufacturer and trust to his mercy, which was
scant.

Of the reports delivered at the convention it was that
of John Brown on "Preparing Wool for Market" which
Wright, in his July, 1847, issue published in full. Brown
described in detail how Americans should wash and tie
up their fleeces to make them marketable in England, for
it was to that trade that he, and the convention, wanted
the wool-growers to turn and thus break the boycott
which the New England mills were apparently going to
bring down upon the cooperative efforts of the rebellious
farmers:

"The greatest hindrance to the sale of American wools
in England and France is the shameful, dishonest practice
of tying up their fleeces with ten and even twenty feet of
small rope, or with strips of bark two or three inches wide,
instead of two or three feet of small twine—wrapping up
coarse and unwashed wool inside some of the finest fleeces
—putting in dirt balls, dirty sweepings of barn floors."

Let farmers be as cleanly about wool as about wheat,
pork and butter and "we should soon have enough of
English and French competitors" to benefit the wool market far more than could any protective tariff. "Our slov-
enly, dishonest habits deprive us of foreign competition,
and leave us entirely at the mercy of our large manufacturing companies—bodies without souls."

Hawk-faced, eagle-eyed, his nose high and his jaw
hard, Brown was speaking words that would be strangely
like those he would be applying, a little later, to another

vested interest, the slave power, which had, as he would charge, no soul whatsoever. Within eight years John Brown would be at war with Slavery on the plains of "Bleeding Kansas," fighting against what he regarded as another of the predatory and vested interests in his country. And within twelve years he would be dead and in two years after that his own soul without its body would be the rolling refrain of one of the world's greatest war songs. And when he would pass into history, only two substantial opinions of him would be held—the South would call him merely an adventurous horse-thief who turned to anti-slavery villainy and national treason as a means of securing funds from Abolitionists—the North would call him a mystic and fanatic who, brooding overlong on the iniquities of human bondage, had lost his mind. Entirely ignored in these two conventional concepts were the arguments he had hurled, as far back as 1847, against financial over-lords, and which revealed him to have been a chronic social reformer.

In the wake of Brown's address, the Steubenville Convention resolved to make his establishment at Springfield its official wool depot and to establish another at Wheeling, Virginia, and to encourage the building of woolen factories in Ohio.

Out in Chicago, Publisher Wright printed in full the proceedings and kept the subject alive by reciting the advantages of the wool depot and urging that one be opened in Illinois. Finally on April 24, 1851, he issued a circular announcing that he would open one himself. In the back reaches of the prairie, so far from market, the manufacturers agents "withhold correct information from the farmer," a deception which the wool depot would halt, since Wright, himself, would represent the wool-growers.

He was building a five-story warehouse on the Chicago River beside a railroad and would soon open it as a wool depot and agricultural warehouse. Opening in time to receive wool from the 1851 clip, he maintained the depot through 1852, issuing a circular which printed scores of letters of commendation from farmers, some of whom extolled him as a public benefactor.

Wright was entering the implement field, and it was partly due to his greater excitement over the reaper that caused him in May, 1853, to abandon the wool depot. But a more significant reason was the improvement in prices paid farmers by the manufacturers. Eager to halt the cooperative trend, the large buyers had begun to deal more fairly with the producers. Brown and Perkins, at the same time, abandoned their wool depot and Brown began to stir with the emotions and decisions that would, in 1855, start him on the road to Kansas, Harper's Ferry, the noose, martyrdom and immortality.

News of John Brown's Raid upon the Harper's Ferry arsenal in 1859 came with tragic impact to the home of John S. Wright in Chicago.

George Washington Turner, Mrs. Wright's older brother, had been living at Rippon not far from Blakeley, when he heard that Black Abolitionists were starting a slave insurrection down at Harper's Ferry. As a retired army officer he had kept bachelor's hall at Rippon, where, when his sister Kitty was nearby, he summoned her to preside over his table on formal occasions. Graduating from West Point in 1831 and serving in the Seminole War he had resigned in 1836 and settled down to the life of a slaveholder and gentleman of leisure. But his military past as well as his interest in slavery had brought him to action on the day of John Brown's Raid and carrying a shotgun he had ridden down into town to receive a bullet through the neck and topple to the ground dead. One story had it that he had been shooting at two of the raiders when the ball struck him; another that he had been talking to a fellow-posseman when Brown's men, firing from the beleaguered arsenal, had hit him. The death of so prominent a citizen, followed within a few minutes by the fall of the town's mayor, fanned the citizens to such fury that when some of the raiders were captured a little later, they were massacred on the spot.

To Kitty Turner Wright who was still vehemently pro-Southern and pro-slavery, this loss was not a battle casualty but plain "murder" and the tragedy might well have been influential in her husband's attitude, so soon to develop after 1859, of refusal to sympathize with a war for the freeing of the slaves.

Never had Wright added the abolition of slavery to his program of reform. He remained aloof, treating the anti-slavery agitation as mere political maneuvering or fanatical excess while so many of his fellow-New Englanders in the West toiled for the cause. His fellow-reformer, Judge Caton, was the prime mover in making Chicago famous—or infamous—as an "Abolition city." Caton enlisted a coppersmith named Allan Pinkerton, at Dundee, to act as agent for Chicago Abolitionists on "The Underground Railway" and thus did much to establish Pinkerton as a detective.

Although it must have been a disappointment to Caton to find the energetic young Wright, who had worked with him so successfully in launching the Union Agricultural Society, failing to go along with the Abolition reform, he never let it modify his admiration of Wright. Years later Caton, as an old man, reviewed his own career as farmer, lawyer, Chief Justice of the Supreme Court of Illinois, land-holder, promoter of an early telegraph, and intimate of practically all the influential men of Illinois for more than two generations; he turned over in his mind many things. Then he said that "as he looked back and noted the successive steps in the progress made in Illinois and the neighboring States during the past fifty years, he, without hesitation, gave John S. Wright the credit of seeing more clearly than anyone else he had known, the possibilities of this part of the country and just what measures must be taken and how to make those possibilities realities." [1]

Caton was thinking of Wright's foresight as to railroads and schools and the hedge fence and fruit trees and analysis of soils, diversification of crops, improved farm implements and the change of the prairie from a grazing range to a closely cultivated region. It was, indeed, Wright's propaganda that would eventually culminate in the victory which Illinois' Legislature decreed in 1874 when it passed the bill making it illegal "for the owner of the horse, ass, mule, cattle, sheep, goat or hog to suffer the same to run at large" and thus putting the burden of fencing upon the grazier and drover, not the husbandman.

Caton might have been thinking of Wright's frequent agitation for farmers, inventors, blacksmiths to make a fence of wire. As early as September, 1845, Wright's paper had recorded the experiments of a farmer, R. L. Allen, near Buffalo, who was making fence with strands of wire, and in November, 1847, it described how the parallel wires strung between posts would behead prairie chickens which flew against it, turn back horses and cattle, but not—not the prairie hog. *The Prairie Farmer* urged more experiments. Some day the wire fence would serve.

It is likely Caton, in his review, missed one of Wright's early demonstrations of foresight—the dairy. Of Wright's contemporaries those who eventually appreciated him failed to include this in their catalog of his pioneerings. It was an unspectacular campaign as compared with many of his others, and was carried on steadily as part of the larger campaign of revolutionizing prairie agricul-

(1) The Educational History of Illinois, by John Williston Cook, Chicago, 1912.

ture. Yet it was one of the most radical of Wright's proposals, since to have an editor urging prairie cattlemen
to raise milk cows was as startling as if some editor of
the 1890s had advised Buffalo Bill to become a milk-maid.

Settlers on the wild prairies in 1841 regarded the milk
cow as a minor contributor to the dinner table, a creature
to be classed with the small vegetable garden as worth
some trifling attention, perhaps, from the women folks
and children, but scarcely up to the notice of the male
horseman who headed the family.

Furthermore it was a tedious job to hunt up milk cows
of a morning, for they would stray indefinitely across the
unfenced range in the night, and their udders often had
caked before they could be found. Sometimes they were
never found at all, sometimes they died, bogged down in
swamps, or were swept up in the herds of wild steers
which drovers from Missouri whooped eastward to the
feeding grounds of Ohio. Then, too, the quality of milk
fell off rapidly after August when the long prairie grass
died on the stem. Also, with the roads little but quagmires,
except in late summer, there was small chance to haul
butter and cheese to market, and such hogs as might have
drunk the skim-milk were off somewhere on the prairies
enjoying the more heroic life of foragers.

But Wright, in his January, 1841, issue had begun his
campaign with laudatory wood-cuts and columns about
the little-known Ayrshire cow, which could produce five
pounds of butter a week. Ignoring the West's fondness
for big cattle which would supply oxen, Wright argued
that cattle shows and fairs were doing disservice in award-
ing all the prizes to "fat and sleeky cattle" and thus de-
preciating the value of milkers.

In his June issue, just six months after he had asked
his readers to tell him what they knew of the Osage
Orange hedge, he asked them what they knew about the

small, milk-producing cows kept by the French farmers in their old colonies in Southern Illinois. Could they be descended from the Alderney dairy cows of France? "If some one will send up information he may render the agricultural community a great favor, for it is said no breed is equal to the Alderney for the dairy."

In his next month's issue he began shaming the West for importing butter and cheese from New York instead of producing its own. "Who will commence the work?" That December saddle-weary cow-barons at night read in *The Prairie Farmer* the demands of a young, city-dwelling editor that the West observe how Eastern Ohio had just sent 500,000 pounds of butter to New York via the Erie Canal. The January number of 1842 predicted that "ten or twenty years hence, when the West begins to give the vast surplus of the dairy business, how small this (500,000 pounds) will appear." A decade before the railroads had arrived, Wright was telling his readers they must prepare for the day.

Wright's handiwork was apparent in the prizes for butter which the Union Agricultural Society included in its premiums at its annual Cattle Show and Fair. The awards were for butter put up in kegs of 50 pounds or more and stored for at least three months prior to exhibition. This would educate farmers to learn to make butter on a scale and quality needed when the time came for them to ship it to the Atlantic States. All exhibits must be accompanied by "a minute description of the processes of manufacture and packing" so that the whole community might benefit.

Wright's paper demanded that the quality of butter be improved by the building of milk houses and cellars—"The dairy woman has perhaps but a single room in a log house for cooking, sleeping and keeping milk and making butter. Under such circumstances we might as well look for alli-

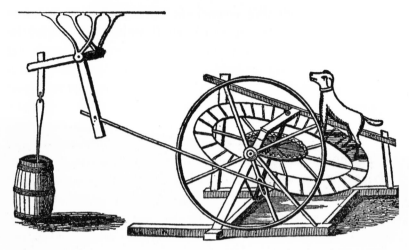

Dog power for churning. From *The Prairie Farmer*, September, 1846.

gators to grow on cotton trees." By February, 1845, the paper was pointing out significantly that butter from cows pastured on cultivated grasses took first prize at fairs, while that from cows fed on the wild, free grasses, came in second best. The first, if carefully worked, could be sold for 15 cents a pound on the Chicago market, the second if indifferently made must go at no better than 6 cents.

Tirelessly the paper examined and published evidence as to the best dairy cows. It was the fall of 1855 Wright first saw the Alderney, or Jersey, as some people called it. He came across specimens near Boston, and in his October, 1855, issue, published pictures and a glowing description of the strange little creatures who "look like a parcel of overgrown fawns . . . a mousey dun mixed with white." They were just what the West wanted—giving only six to twelve quarts of milk a day but "ten quarts will make as much butter as twenty-two of ordinary cows" so rich was the quality.

Higher profits, Western pride, the wisdom of having

many irons in the fire instead of entrusting everything to one crop, many were the strings to the bow with which Wright sought to charm the prairie settler into becoming a dairyman-farmer. And in his paper's part in the victory which was eventually won, much was due to Ambrose Wight's success in pursuing one of Wright's early policies —the enlisting of women on the side of the reformers.

Ambrose Wight had enlarged the paper's capacity for supplying household remedies, cooking recipes, domestic advice for the women alongside veterinarian counsel for the male stock-raisers. The paper admonished women not to wear calico dresses in winter lest they share "the horrible deaths occasioned by their taking fire" at open hearths. It urged women to demand ice houses for butter and milk and for the cure of bilious attacks. It campaigned for wind pumps in the middle '40s and, in April, 1847, asked why farmers couldn't have ice cream freezers as well as people in the cities, and gave directions for their manufacture at home. It warned farm boys and girls to avoid the temptations of the city, campaigned steadily for temperance after Wight's arrival, and asked farmers' daughters what would become of the dairy industry if they kept rushing off to the factories to become "milliners, sewers, shoe-binders or straw-braiders?"

The paper did not, however, join as energetically as did some of its rivals in the campaign which male farmers waged, through the 1850s, to keep their women folks on the milking stool.

Encouraged by the agitation for Women's Rights, one of the many reforms advocated during the period, some farm women had begun to question the ancient tradition that milking a cow was peculiarly work for female hands. In the New World where democracy and equality were supposed to flower, women had already been freed, in general, from the Old World task of hoeing in the fields and, listening to what gallant males said about the new position the fair sex was holding, began to think that now was the time to do away with that inherited institution—the milk-maid.

Suddenly facing the prospect of having to do the tedious chore themselves, the farmers protested, objected and then finally summoning science to their aid, got farm papers to publish a most ingenious argument:

Cream rose to the top of milk in crocks, didn't it? Well then, the same thing must be true in the cow's udder; the richest milk was the last to be drawn out by the hand of the milker. It was these "strippings" that made the best butter and cheese.

However, the cow if displeased with her milker, had it in her power to hold back and not give all her milk down. The hard and calloused hands of the farmer hurt the cow's teats; she flinched; sometimes she kicked the bucket galley-west, and usually she withheld the last and best portions of her supply.

But let her be milked by the gentle hands of women, and she made her contribution with contented alacrity. Women were superior creatures anyway—ministering angels; everybody said that. And kindness, not to speak of economy, required that the work be done by them and them alone.

Before such flattery, the social revolution died—the storm went around—and the farm woman again sat down upon the milking stool.

As the nation grew richer in the middle 1850s, and the cities grew, discussions of etiquette crept into Wright's paper, a writer signing herself Nellie Grey, advising girls, in the May, 1855, issue:

"Don't go into a fit of the hips every time you see a hat and a pair of whiskers. Don't get it into your head that you must put yourself in the way of every young

man in the neighborhood in order to attract notice, for
if you don't run after the men, they will run after you.
Mark that?"

"I am a woman's rights man, too," wrote a male, sheltering himself behind the pen name "Celes" in the December, 1857, issue. "If a young lady has a particular wish
to see a young gentleman who does not see fit or hasn't
the time to call on her, why it is the most natural thing in
the world that she should at a proper time call on him.
She should, however, take special care that she make not
her visit at such unpropitious occasions as those when
young men are feeding the hogs, or butchering the beef, or
drawing out manure. Love chats on such occasions would
be sadly ill-timed—probably unsuccessful."

That woman's daily happiness, as well as the price of
her husband's property on the great bare prairies would
be improved by shade and fruit trees was a truism that
Wright's paper never let the West forget. As early as
April, 1845, it was publishing complete directions and illustrations on grafting and budding fruit trees.

To widen the diet of the log-cabin dwellers was a duty
with the paper, and frequently it jolted Chicagoans, as in
October, 1844, when it said "Of garden fruits such as cur-
rants, gooseberries, raspberries and strawberries, ripe gi-
raffes would scarcely be a greater novelty in our markets."

Furthest in advance of the time, however, was the
paper's campaign from 1843 onward for the substitution of
broiling for frying.

"It is impossible that heavy-half-cooked bread, meat
fried to the dryness and toughness of Manila rope . . .
can be taken into the stomach habitually without injury.
. . . Does anyone know how much the tendency of our
climate toward bilious and intermittent fevers is favored
by the habits of a part of our Western population of eating
warm bread and drinking strong coffee and eating a large

proportion of animal food without fruit or vegetables. . . . Oh, of how much family discord has bad cooking been productive." One correspondent, catching the crusade, wrote for the November, 1845, issue, "In the West it is fry, dry, fry; all food is fried and dished floating in villainous liquid grease and dirt. . . . Such food accounts for much of the disease of the country."

In a day when it was commonly accepted that food on the farm was far better than "the withered dainties" of the city, and that the plowman had glorious and ruddy health while his city cousin was pale and sluggish, *The Prairie Farmer* was arguing to the contrary. Its editors had discovered in the reports of the 1850 census that the nation's highest mortality was in the rural, not the urban, regions of Massachusetts. This argued that salted meats were to blame, since the Bay State farmers had, for generations, specialized on this diet.

The settler on the prairie was in the same predicament, since, for what the paper described as "eight months of the year," he had no meat but salt meat. With no ice houses to provide refrigeration, he dared butcher no steer, sheep or pig, from March to late in October, lest a warm spell spoil the unconsumed part of the meat. On the thinly settled prairie he had insufficient neighbors to make "the trading of meat" possible. He was, as the paper said, "isolated from city or village markets." All that he could do was to butcher in November, December, January or February, and salt down meat for use in the spring, summer and fall.

So steady a diet not only overdosed the human system with salt, it so sickened "the females of the family that they refused salt meat almost wholly," and grew pale from the very lack of nourishing food. Although physicians as a group fought this rural debility with liberal doses of calomel and of drastic purgatives, *The Prairie*

Farmer in January, 1854, produced a Chicago physician who, like the paper itself, had ideas far in advance of his day. He had found that young people coming to Chicago from the farm were often "poorly" because their appetites had been ruined by this salt meat diet. He had been "uniformly successful," he said, in merely prescribing for them "something to eat," and by providing a diversified diet feasible in a city of Chicago's size.

The editors seconded him with a prescription of their own—raise roosters and eat them. "He can be killed in the morning and eaten at noon as easily as an apple can be plucked." Do this, and rural ill-health would be revolutionized!

One of the paper's most diligent searches was for devices which would do away with the plague of rats. For years after the arrival of emigrants in Northern Illinois, the rodents had been scarce and "even as late as 1843 they had not penetrated inland as far as Rock River in Winnebago county . . . although plenty enough in the Lake towns." By the early 1850s, however, complaints were legion all over the upper half of the State, farmers maintaining that the rats had worked their way inland from Chicago which was forever swarming with them. Month by month the paper published schemes for their eradication—simple purges such as powders which blew up inside the animal, the loud beating of drums around the house of nights, the baiting of fish-hooks hung high so that the rat might be suspended when he had leaped too surely, the insertion into rat-holes of "The Fairy Compound," a mixture of lard, phosphorous and whiskey in pellet form. For a time it was hoped that the right thing was "to catch one and singe him, or tie a bell to him, or abuse him in some way, when all his relations will take to their heels and be seen no more." Then came a wave of loosing pet coons and weasels upon the rodents, but both insisted upon killing more chickens than rats.

One correspondent from Chemung, Illinois, told in the May, 1855, issue how "the suck-egg gentry" had overwhelmed his henhouse, barns and dwelling in nighttime guerilla raids until "someone told me that he had heard someone else say that the Guinea Fowl would drive away rats." He bought some guineas "and as soon as I got the buckwheat music going, Messrs. Rat began to march—off; and for something over two years I have neither seen nor heard a rat around my premises."

Elaborate traps were described, one, in the October, 1855, number, being a barrel covered with a tight sheep skin sliced at right angles in the center and smeared with grease and meal. When a convenient ramp was arranged, the rat ventured up and out onto the skin, which let him plop into water below. Down there, however, he found an island refuge in the form of a brick upon which he was supposed to climb "and thereupon to set up a cry which will call the whole family of rats to see what the matter is. As each newcomer enters on the skin-covered top, he, too, is plunged below to keep company with the alarmist."

Although *The Prairie Farmer's* greatest pioneering in the livestock field was in the awakening of the West to the Jersey and other milk breeds, it did pound steadily at the value of blooded stock in the beef strains.

That Chicago was to be a great packing center as soon as the lake traffic and railroads became extensive, was preached early and often by Wright. In 1834, two years after his arrival in Chicago as a boy, he had seen Sylvester Marsh swinging beeves from an oak limb and packing beef to ship east via the vagrant steamers or by the stages which strained slowly eastward. After that the packing industry grew till by November, 1848, *The Prairie Farmer* was recording how Wadsworth, Dyer & Co., the largest firm of the kind in Chicago, was packing in salt "for the

English market only at $10 per tierce—all they can deliver.
... They will slaughter about 3,500 this season, and employ
70 to 80 men."

It was a great waste, *The Prairie Farmer* pointed
out, that "the hundreds of loads of bones, blood, manure,
livers, lungs and shreds" were thrown away when they
should go back to the land as manure.

Whether the paper's comments on the subject were
wholly or only partially responsible for a reform in this
matter, the fact remains that in the December issue of
1850—two years later—it declared that the offal from the
largely increased activities of the packers was being carted
to Bridgeport, a suburb, and fed to swine, although "the
blood is discharged into the river and is the only loss. "Can
it not be made available for sugar refining and dyeing or
something else? The manure, instead of going the same
way with the blood, as it has done, awaits the winter, when
it is thrown on the land."

By 1849 the paper was exulting, "Chicago is the first
point in the United States for slaughtering and putting up
beef. There are some two or three establishments engaged in this business here, who have no rivals in the
United States." The thing Wright had urged from the
beginning, the delivery of livestock to the Chicago market
was coming true, and by December, 1851, soon after the
Galena and Chicago railroad had begun to be effective,
the city's beef packers, eight in number, were thriving,
employing 463 hands and killing 30,000 animals.

So exuberant did the prairies become that an Illinois
cattle-fattener, F. H. Miner, declared in the January, 1851,
issue of *The Prairie Farmer* that "Chicago beef is better than Eastern because it is produced from pure air and
healthy food," the cattle being free from the necessity, so
universal in the East, of eating grass which they had
themselves manured.

In 1848 success was visible in the campaign against razor-back hogs; the average animal sold in Chicago weighed not less than 300 pounds, an increase of fifty per cent in five years. Here and there across the prairie, farmers were finding that clover and corn in 18 months, could produce a hog weighing 370 pounds.

True to Wright's predictions and his paper's constant advocacy, Chicago forged ahead in pork packing, "barrelling" 16,000 animals in the winter of 1849-50, although still far behind Springfield's 18,500, Pekin's 25,000, Peoria's 21,000, Beardstown's 31,000, Terre Haute's 65,000, not to speak of Cincinnati's 406,000. But by 1859, when the railroads had established Chicago as the transportation center of the Northwest, the city had climbed to third place among pork-packers of the West, and in the winter 1864-65 its slaughter of 900,000 hogs within three months gave it first place in the nation—three times Cincinnati's figure.

The AMERICAN HOG TAMER

PATENTED BY R. HURD, April 11, 1862.
— T O —

Fatten and Prevent Hogs Rooting!

Before pigs noses were "ringed" with wire to curb their destructive "rooting" the above method of cutting a triangle of flesh in their noses was widely advertised. From *The Prairie Farmer*, April 9, 1864.

CHAPTER XII

The Poor Man's Fence

ALTHOUGH it was John S. Wright who first made significant suggestion of the Osage Orange hedge and the Agricultural University to the prairie people, it was not he, but Professor Jonathan B. Turner of Jacksonville whom they would remember, generations later, as the "father" of those two epochal institutions.

As brother reformers, Wright and Turner had much in common although their personal intimacy was never great. Each had come from New England in the early '30s, fresh from classical studies. Turner had preached in New England for a short time before migrating on his mission Westward, and had combined preaching and teaching at Jacksonville, Illinois, till 1848 when his objections to his brother-clerics' conservatism on slavery and on orthodox religion prompted him to resign both pulpit and classroom.

Both Turner and Wright were always subject to the evangelistic impulse; each fought unselfishly for better schools as for the propagation of a great faith. Turner, nearer to fanaticism, remained poor all his life, never attempting as did Wright to roll up a fortune so that he might, among other pleasures, endow educational projects. Single-tracked of mind where Wright was catholic, sarcastic where Wright was only stormy, then gentle, Turner fought for school reforms with a challenging pen, Wright with a contagious enthusiasm.

Each wrote with fiery eloquence when deeply stirred,

but where Wright was never able to stick long enough to a subject to master its intricacies, Turner was a patient scientist.

Both were mystics, called "cranks" by their neighbors. But while Wright went no further than the field of ecstatic prophecy about cities and regions, Turner believed in spiritualism and mental telepathy and wrote pamphlets on metaphysical subjects. Wright urged farmers to solve their problems by their own efforts; Turner experimented on his own farm at Jacksonville, studying insects with a microscope, analyzing soils, rotating crops, and inventing farm implements. His was among the first of the mechanical corn-planters, and he took out patents on various weeders and cultivators.

Public morals interested Turner far more than Wright, and the professor's pen flayed the Mormons most intemperately in one of the several pamphlets he issued. Another of his publications assailed Slavery with true Abolitionist fervor. Wright, craving national unity, favored keeping Slavery where, and as, it was.

Turner courted Wright's favor and made *The Prairie Farmer* the chief medium for his campaigns for progress in fencing and education.

Some twenty years after his arrival in Illinois, Turner described in Wright's paper how "from the first time I rode over these beautiful prairies for some thousand miles on horseback, and slept sometimes on my saddle for a pillow—without food or blanket—I have never had but those two ideas in my head. . . . But two things were needed for this State to make it the very first State in the civilized world, viz.:

"1. A feasible and easy mode of enclosing its rich soils.

"2. A practical and feasible mode of educating all the people." [1]

(1) Prairie Farmer, March, 1852.

The more he saw of the prairie the more he "was led to see the utter impossibility of a proper social organization of society, so long as the want of fencing material compelled the people to form broken and scattered settlements on the margins of groves and streams, while all within was left a solitary waste. . . . I then thought that the greatest moral, intellectual, social and pecuniary benefactor would be the man who should first devise some feasible mode of fencing. Accordingly . . . I commenced a series of experiments with hedge plants."(²)

Like a man possessed, he began filling the acre and a half, which he owned, with whatever plants might conceivably turn out to be the "poor man's fence," anything that might prove "horse-high, bull-strong and pig-tight."

He scoured the agricultural papers, the botanical encyclopedias, he wrote to friends in all parts of the country, he talked to everybody he saw. By 1852 he had tested in succession and found wanting, the black locust, the thorn locust, the black walnut, the poplar, cottonwood, mulberry, privet, gooseberry, sweet briar, crabapple, wild rose, English thorn, Alabama rose, Scotch furze, arbor vitae, and several native American thorns.

Then one day in the summer of 1835, when he had been sitting in a camp meeting at Pisgah, Illinois, God had seemed to come to his assistance.

Turner had been, like the rest of the congregation, bored almost beyond endurance by the tedious sermon of a formal, broadclothed, orthodox cleric from New York. Indeed, the young people had slid off the split-log benches and had stolen out in the woods, presumably to pick blackberries. Turner's mind, always impatient with the "over-educated," strayed, too, and as the long afternoon wore on, he was in the midst of a day-dream when a dusty, disheveled and almost ragged man caught his eye. The fellow

(2) Hedges, by Prof. J. B. Turner, Prairie Farmer, November, 1847.

was striding up the grassy aisle of the open air meeting, with a worn shoe on one foot and a tattered boot on the other. Assuming the man to be some vagrant, blundering into the wrong place, Turner reached out and stopped him.

But even as he did so the elegant preacher stopped his monotonous lecture and, springing down from the crude pulpit, rushed to take the stranger's hand, and then to introduce him as the Rev. Dr. David Nelson, head rider of the circuit of Illinois, Kentucky, Tennessee, Arkansas and Missouri. Led to the pulpit, the famous divine began speaking, the congregation woke up, the young people deserted blackberries and Cupid, and soon the benches were full. For three hours the people sat spell-bound as Nelson warned them of hell and promised salvation.

When the service was done, Turner took Nelson home with him, and they talked far into the night. "I expressed my views to him freely," Turner recalled later on, "especially as regards the social and religious advantages of closer settlements among our Western people." Turner explained why he was hunting so desperately for a hedge fence. Had Nelson in his travels seen any plant that might possibly serve?

"He told me," said Turner, "he had seen a plant in the wilds of the far South, which, if it could be procured and acclimated, he had not the least doubt would answer our purpose." The only trouble was that the old circuit-rider couldn't remember the name of the plant, and for the next four years Turner wrote everybody who might know of it, sending letters right and left "both in the United States and Texas." Finally he saw in an agricultural paper an article by a Colonel MacDonald of Alabama on a hedge called the "Maclura." It sounded like the Reverend Nelson's plant, and, writing to the Colonel, Turner procured "one simple plant" as he remembered "for which I paid, I think, one dollar."

"The moment I saw it I was satisfied it was precisely the thing if it could be made to stand the climate and not run up at the top or sprout at the root."

Setting out a hedge of the precious plants in 1839 he watched and tended them with passionate zeal, saying nothing about his hopes, however, and waiting, like a true scientist, for proof before he made any announcement.

Up in Chicago, John S. Wright, knowing nothing of Turner's experiments, had come upon a description of the same plant in an old magazine, and had immediately seized upon it as the thing that might well solve the great problem of fencing the prairie.

While preparing copy in the autumn of 1840 for his first formal issue of the *Union Agriculturalist*, he had spent days, scissors in hand, studying the back numbers of Eastern farm papers. A sentence caught his eye in the *Hartford Silk Culturalist*, the organ of the faddists who had been caught up in the "Silk Mania"—a dream that the United States could become a nation of silk producers, with worms feeding on mulberry leaves all summer in the back yard and surrendering long threads of silk to farm women in attics all winter.

The magazine, in discussing various substitutes for the mulberry, mentioned that there might be splendid worm-food in the foliage of the Osage Orange, or the Maclura, as it had been scientifically named for its "discoverer" Dr. William Maclure, the geologist. As President of the Philadelphia Academy of Natural History, surveyor and explorer in the United States, Spain, the West Indies and Mexico, McClure had in 1825 made vain efforts to start an agricultural school at the communal colony in New Harmony, Indiana, so near the great prairies of Illinois.

The Maclura was a native of Arkansas where the Indians called it "Bow Wood" because its branches made tough and springy hunting weapons. The French, passing through the region, called it "Bois D'Arc," a name soon corrupted by American settlers into "Bowdark." Since the plant was of the mulberry family, the hope that it would feed silk-worms was only as vain as was the "silk mania" itself. What was important to Wright was that the *Horticulturist's* article declared, in passing, that the Osage Orange trees, "when set at a distance of fifteen inches asunder, make the most beautiful as well as the strongest hedge fence in the world, through which neither man nor animals can pass." Reprinting the item in his January, 1841, issue, Wright asked, "Can any one tell us more of this tree? . . . it seems well adapted . . . and if any has been used in Missouri or elsewhere, it would be a great favor to have an account of it furnished to us."

There was no response. In the May issue he printed a description he had found in another old magazine and added, "It seems to be a most excellent material for hedges and if there is seed to be obtained anywhere or if anyone can give directions for procuring it, I should very much like to have it." Almost a year later when a farmer, B. F. Lodge, in Edgar county, wrote that he had been trying it out, Wright passed the information on to his readers, with the observation, "Ever since the first number we have been trying to learn something relative to the Osage Orange, but hitherto without success."

Even when such authorities as Solon Robinson wrote to him that "Hedges will never fence the prairies; they are too subject to blight," Wright answered in the March, 1842, issue that the critics were talking about the imported hedges; he, himself was convinced more strongly than ever that the right hedge would be found among the native shrubs. "Our views of its practicability and importance to the West are not changed; we still think it is to be our chief means of fencing."

When one farmer suggested the cottonwood, Wright

declared that "something not quite so old-maidish would look better"; the cottonwood had "too much primness and mustn't-touch-me sort of air." Month by month he printed settlers' descriptions of their experiments with many kinds of picket, paling, log and board fences, finding each a failure because of the same old shortage of lumber. For a time high hopes were held for a system of earthen ramparts fronted by deep ditches—six feet from foot to crown, but the intrepid "land-shark" hogs went up and over the battlements with the same triumphant flourish of a pigtail that Wellington's grenadiers had given in the Napoleonic Wars.

With the advent of J. Ambrose Wight in 1843, Wright concentrated on educational news and his associate for a time did nothing more aggressive than publish the letters of farmers who kept up the struggle to find the right fence.

When Charles H. Larrabee, later a judge in Wisconsin, stopped in at *The Prairie Farmer* office one day late in 1844 and handed over some Osage Orange seed, saying that he had seen it growing in Arkansas and that it would be "a good hedge for Illinois and Wisconsin," Ambrose Wight planted the seed near the office, but neglected the plants when they came up, and they soon died. Furthermore that same year, Wight visited Turner's home at Jacksonville and saw the progress the Professor was making with the Maclura, but failed to be impressed. A born conservative and a narrowly religious man, familiar with the controversies which plagued his friends, the orthodox clergy, on the frontier, he was no one to be sympathetic with a "rebel" and possibly a "heretic" like Professor Turner, who that year was quitting Illinois College and the ministry because both seemed too reactionary.

Ambrose Wight had already settled upon the buckthorn hedge as his candidate for the honor of fencing the prairies, and he was probably offended at Turner's decision that it wouldn't do.

Turner, himself, was not ready for publicity on his experiments, and as late as December, 1845, was telling *The Prairie Farmer* readers that while he had proved the Osage Orange would stand the northern climate, he wasn't yet convinced the plants would "grow close enough together to form a good hedge." And he held to his refusal to endorse the Maclura even though a storm of requests for seed poured in on him following his December article. His scientific soul must be satisfied.

That he was depending upon Wright's paper as his medium was indicated by a letter he wrote on December 1, 1846, to Augustus H. Higgins of Petersburg, Illinois: "The Prairie Farmer is the only journal of education published in our State, so far as I know; it is issued, as you are aware, from Chicago; and aside from its department on education, it is one of the best agricultural papers in the Union, and the only one I now take."[3]

Through 1846 and '47 he kept trying to stop the rush of the curious by informing them through *The Prairie Farmer* of his inability to yet assure them the hedge would stop the rapacious razorbacks. He told them how he had sent to Texas for two million seed in '47 and how these had all come up in '48, giving him enough plants to complete the enclosure of some twelve or thirteen acres. That year he sent for enough more seed to equip eight Illinois nurserymen, making them promise first that they would sell to the public at from $5 to $10 per thousand, no more, no less.[4] Three or four years before, the price in the East had been $500 per thousand, but had now fallen to $12 since various Eastern agricultural journals had begun recommending the plant to farmers.

(3) Turner letter, Illinois State Historical Library.
(4) Turner in Prairie Farmer, August, 1848.

Never had Turner "been able for one moment to persuade himself that the beneficent Creator had committed the obvious blunder of making the prairies without also making something to fence them with . . . and if all men should fail for a hundred years to come to make the discovery, I should still believe that God had somewhere on this continent produced a shrub which he designed especially for the purpose of fencing the prairies."(5)

By August, 1848, he was telling the paper's readers that the Osage Orange "*is* that shrub, and the greatest blessing ever introduced upon the farms of the West," and in the November number he announced he was now ready to sell plants at a price that would permit the fencing of 80 rods for not more than $15. The minimum for "a good post and board fence" built at a point remote from timber was put by one correspondent at $100 for a similar distance.(6) So rapidly did seed pour into the country that Turner advised *Prairie Farmer* readers in the October, 1853, issue that the price was now down to a point where 80 rods of Osage Orange would cost only $7.50 as against $75 in either rail or picket fencing. Moreover, if a rail fence escaped the prairie fires, it would still wear out in twelve years, whereas the Maclura fence, if trimmed with a "splasher" (half a mile a day by a green hand, a mile a day by an expert) would be stronger than ever at the end of twelve summers.

"I now write" Turner told the readers of that October issue, "with my eye resting upon a hedge four years old . . . on the public street through which thousands of mules and wild Missouri steers, hogs and sheep are driven each year and all the stock of this village runs at large. And Pharaoh of old knew what a starved town cow was." Behind this hedge lay all Turner's fruit trees and gardens, yet "the wild Missouri steers will not throw it down or bulge over in droves

(5) Ibid.   (6) "J. G." in Prairie Farmer, April, 1855.

... as they used to do every year before I had a hedge."

Now that it was established, he proposed that it be called just "The Prairie Hedge Plant" since "It is our plant —God made it for us, and we will call it by the name of our 'green ocean home'."

That Turner should be hailed as the "father" of the sensational discovery, irked Ambrose Wight, and in the June, 1855, number he declared "it is perfectly ridiculous to assert, as many are in the habit of doing, that this or that man introduced the Osage Orange as a hedge plant." Going back across the files of the paper he was able to show how John S. Wright had begun the agitation for it, and how often his columns had discussed it before Professor Turner had made his appearance in print. He thought Alexander J. Downing, writing in his *Horticulturist*, an Eastern publication, had made the plant a national sensation by commending it along with the buckthorn in February, 1847, and that a wealthy Ohio horticultural zealot, William Neff, had made the first "extended and accurate experiments." Professor Turner, he admitted, had "undoubtedly done more than any other man to get it to the notice of the farmers of our State" due principally to "his elegantly written articles" which "were put forth in the columns of this paper."

Neither Wright nor Turner took official notice of the controversy which ensued, with champions of the latter snowing Ambrose Wight under with facts and arguments supporting the general belief of the farmers that it had been the Professor who had given them the fence which was destined to be one of the major reasons for Illinois increasing its population more than 100 per cent in the decade of the '50s—rising from eleventh place among the States in 1850 to third in 1860.

Ambrose Wight was in no frame of mind to do Turner justice, for between them had risen still another issue—the Agricultural University, which, like the Osage Orange, John S. Wright, the editor, had first suggested for the prairies and which Turner, the practical experimenter, had more recently made his own project.

Among the countless agricultural inventions of the 1850s and '60s was this elaborate machine for husking corn—ingenious but destined never to be popular. From *The Prairie Farmer*, August 26, 1858.

CHAPTER XIII

"A Sort of Scientific University"

WITH Chicago booming and his real estate rising in value, Wright sat down at his desk in the spring of 1849 and wrote an announcement for the May issue of his paper:

"It has ever been my intention to devote the profits of The Prairie Farmer to the cause of education as soon as I could afford to relinquish them. The advertising now yields about $1,200, which I will now retain to myself for the present, and the entire profit on subscriptions shall be used to promote *education in the West*. The expenses of publication, including one year's salary, are about $3,300, and the subscriptions promptly paid will yield $300 to $500 net. One-half the sale of back numbers shall be given, and as soon as about $1,000 of indebtedness on the paper is paid, the whole receipts from this source shall be used in like manner.

"Many friends of The Prairie Farmer are active promoters of education, and this proposition is made to induce them to still greater efforts to extend the circulation of the paper. . . . To enlarge the Educational Department would be one of the most effectual methods that could be adopted to advance the general cause of education throughout the West."

Even while he was receiving congratulations upon his philanthropy, complications set in. Ambrose Wight had decided he could give only part time to *The Prairie Farmer*. Religion, always so powerful in Wight's mind, was drawing him away, and a remarkable newcomer to Chicago, William Bross, was offering him another job.

The worst of it was that admiration for John S. Wright had brought Bross into the picture.

Out walking on the prairie south of Chicago, one day in the previous year, Wright had met a group of immigrants plodding toward the city on foot. They had left the Michigan Central train, the day before, at its Western terminus, Kalamazoo, and had taken the stage, "a cross between a coach and a lumber box," for the rest of the journey. However, the roughness of the road had so covered them with "bangs and bruises" that by sun-up they had decided to walk.

William Bross had been one of them, a New Englander with literary leanings, and with so much religion in him that he would soon be known to Chicago as "Deacon." He fell into conversation with Wright as they walked, and always afterward he remembered how graciously Wright "gave me a cordial welcome and a great deal of valuable information." The editor took Bross to church on Sunday, introduced him to Mayor Woodworth and other leading citizens, "giving me a lesson in courtesy which I have never forgotten."

Wright's impress on Bross was immediate and emphatic. After a few months as a partner in a book store, Bross sold out and became, like his model, an editor and publisher. It was only a little religious paper, the *Herald of the Prairies*, organ of the Western Presbyterians and Congregationalists, that he bought, but it was a start, and to partake as much as possible of John S. Wright's established success in the publishing field, Bross persuaded Ambrose Wight to become his partner, and, as a side-line, to edit the church paper from his *Prairie Farmer* desk. This gave Bross, who handled the business affairs of the new venture, a chance to sit in *The Prairie Farmer* office,

too, and study John S. Wright at first hand. He thought
then, as later, that Wright was "one of the most enter-
prising and valuable citizens Chicago ever had."

Even when, after a few months, it was plain that the
religious paper was unprofitable, Bross, in selling out to
Ambrose Wight in November, 1851, managed to be kept
on in the office at $1 a day.

By the time he left, in September, 1852, to join John L.
Scripps in starting another newspaper, the *Democratic
Press*, Bross had mastered Wright's technique in the art
of enlivening statistics with prophecy, and soon he was
rivalling his teacher in crying aloud the manifest destiny
of Chicago. Bross' influence widened, a little later, when he
and his paper were incorporated into the *Chicago Tribune*.

With Ambrose Wight tied to his desk by two jobs, *The
Prairie Farmer* was now without the thing that Wright
had always insisted upon—an editor to visit the farmers
over the State. In 1850 he engaged Luther Haven for that
purpose, giving him an interest in the paper, but Haven
left much to be desired, and the worst happened late in
1851, when Ambrose Wight gave notice that in June, he
must give all his time to the *Herald of the Prairies*.

While Wright was looking for someone to take Ambrose Wight's place, "The Old Doctor," John Kennicott—
the little man who looked like a monkey on a horse when
riding the medical circuit—suddenly began to write many
letters to the paper urging new action on schools.

Some years before, "The Old Doctor" had quit practic-
ing medicine and had begun devoting himself to his nursery, interspersed, since 1847, with occasional articles for
The Prairie Farmer on horticulture. But his contacts with
the paper had usually been by mail, for neither his health
nor his wishes prompted him to make many of the 20 mile
trips over villainous roads from Northfield to Chicago. He
had known Wright best through the latter's close friend-

ship with his brother, Hiram who, as owner of a 1,000-acre farm close by, was a great host, and lover of games, one of which, chess, had brought him into companionship with Wright at the Chicago Chess Club. Wright and his family became frequent and long-staying guests at Hiram's home, "The Folly" which stood where, a century later, Arlington Race Track would flourish.

Hiram, who had been Lake county's chief pioneer in the 1830s, had lost his first farm in the panic of '37 and had moved to New Orleans to practice law and garner fat fees. But he had been unable to resist the charm of his old Illinois home and, in 1843, had pulled up stakes and moved back even though his brothers argued that the move was foolish. He had put his wealth into the 960 acres which a settler named Morrison wanted to sell so that he could go to Chicago and start a hotel—one, incidentally, which bore his name, a century later.

"The Folly" consisted of a brick house of twenty rooms, lavishly laid-out grounds, orchards, croquet lawns, big barns adjoining, surrounded by the spacious, rolling acres of his huge farm. What with his twelve children, his wife's friends, his own, and all the brothers, sisters, nephews and nieces of the surrounding Kennicott clan coming and going, "The Folly" was as famous for its hospitality as the neighboring "Grove" was for learning, trees, flowers, fruits and berries. Guests often stayed for weeks, so free and easy was the atmosphere, and so epicurean the table. As time went on, Hiram grew patriarchal, indeed, his round face beaming with good humor as grandchildren, grandnieces and grandnephews, totalling fifty, raced in and out.

The intimacy between Hiram and John S. Wright may well have suggested to Wright that "The Old Doctor" might be the man to fill Ambrose Wight's shoes. But it is more likely that it was "The Old Doctor's" enthusiasm for the newest of Wright's educational proposals, one made in the October, 1851, issue. In a resurgence of his campaign for a State Normal School, Wright had taken a new tack.

Reminding the farmers how they had been lectured for a full decade on their need for agricultural education, he asked them if anything had ever been done. Educators would do nothing, and legislators should not be blamed for doing the same so long as "their applicants did not know what to ask for."

Returning to the idea of an agricultural school which he had proposed in 1843 to the Union Agricultural Society, Wright said: "We think we can see what is needed. A sort of Scientific University where agriculture and all its related sciences shall be thoroughly mastered in the same manner as law, or divinity, or medicine are now mastered in their respective educational institutions." The University would serve as an Agricultural Normal School, equipping teachers to go out and diffuse practical education through the common schools for the benefit of those sons of farmers and mechanics who wished to follow in their fathers' footsteps, yet go beyond them.

"Will the time not come when the farmer will be as intelligent in all that relates to the interior of his profession as the physician is to his?" Wright asked.

By a curious coincidence, Professor Turner, who had been silently studying the Osage Orange hedge at Jacksonville when John S. Wright had proposed it in January, 1841, was formulating a plan for a State Agricultural University when he read Wright proposing virtually the same thing in October, 1851.

As early as May 13, 1841, Turner had spoken on the subject at a Teachers' Institute at Griggsville, Illinois, and on November 18, some six weeks after the October *Prairie Farmer* had been delivered to him, he had read his more

carefully worked out "Plan" at a farmers' meeting at
Granville, Illinois. Its reception had been thrilling; resolutions were adopted demanding a State University for
"all the industrial classes of our State."

Home from the event, Turner wrote *The Prairie
Farmer*, dating his letter "November, 1851":

"Messrs. Editors: I can hardly express to you how much
gratification I derived from the perusal of your editorial.
. . . Without knowing it, you have herein expressed the
same thought and principles that I have cherished for
many years, and not infrequently advanced in addresses
and lectures in this part of the state. I am rejoiced that
without any intercourse with me on the subject, your own
mind, with all your opportunities for conference and observation, has come substantially to the same conclusions,
because it gives me and all others an additional proof that
our views and principles are correct and well founded in
unerring truth. I trust that now you have so well begun,
you will never stop, till we all realize, in some good measure, at least our hearts' desire for the industrial classes."

He added that at the Granville Convention he "was
glad to hear all the members . . . speak of you and your
labors in this cause as you deserve." He enclosed copies of
the proceedings and of his own speech on the "Plan" and
mentioned, significantly, that he hoped all *The Prairie
Farmer* subscribers would re-read carefully the October
editorial "and also the proceedings of this convention,
when they shall come before them."

Feeling that he and the paper were one on the matter,
he sat back, confident that his "Plan" would be spread all
over its columns. But when the January number merely
printed his November letter and a short digest of the
Granville resolutions with no mention of his great address,
he took hot offense. To him the support of the paper was
of primary importance and he quickly empowered his

friend, Dr. Kennicott, to warn the editors that if they opposed his Plan he and his friends would start a rival paper
with "The Old Doctor" as editor.(1)

A great admirer of Turner's ideas on education and the
Osage Orange hedge, Kennicott worked diplomatically to
make peace and to avoid so drastic a show-down. Turner
had been self-centered almost to the point of stupidity in
failing to see why his address had antagonized the editors.
Not only had his Plan proposed financing the Industrial
University with the State's College and Seminary Fund,
but it had declared it "a mean, if not illegal perversion of
this fund to use it for any other purpose." Evidently he
had forgotten how John S. Wright had, for years, campaigned to have this fund devoted to the Normal School.

Likewise, Turner had affronted the orthodox religion-
ist, Ambrose Wight, when he had warned the laboring
classes that the move for a non-sectarian, State-supported
Industrial University would be opposed by the established
colleges which were church-supported and which wanted
funds for themselves. Turner had been brilliantly sarcastic in charging that the cleric-pedagogues who managed the colleges were interested only in educating the
sons of the professional classes so that the doctor-lawyer-
preacher-rich merchant group might preserve its power
over the workers.

Nevertheless, *The Prairie Farmer* did publish Turner's
Plan in its February issue, and after receiving a flood of
sympathy and advice from Kennicott, Turner wrote for
the March number a letter of notable appeasement to John
S. Wright, declaring that if the farmers and their friends
would all pull together, now, as one man, he was satisfied "they can speedily secure for this state and for each
state in the Union, an appropriation of public lands adequate to create and endow in the most liberal manner,

(1) Turner-Kennicott correspondence, Turner Papers, Illinois State Historical
Library.

a general system of popular Industrial Education . . ."

In thus switching his scheme for financing the project, Turner made the first public proposal for the land grant which was subsequently used by Congress to finance the nation-wide system of State Universities.([2]) And it was as the Illinois Industrial University that Turner's state received its "land grant college" in 1867, the name being changed to University of Illinois in 1885.

But Turner would make no such concessions to mollify Ambrose Wight, and both he and Kennicott boiled when Wight, in the March issue, damned the Plan with faint praise and urged that so radical an idea be held in abeyance till older States like Massachusetts and New York had taken action on it.

Then in June, Kennicott was suddenly informed that Ambrose Wight was resigning, and that John S. Wright was taking more active editorial charge. "We shall carry the Plan yet," wrote "The Old Doctor" to Kennicott, and he sent Wright a friendly letter which appeared in the June issue declaring that the paper, as "the only legitimate organ of the producers of Illinois" would be mainly responsible for the victory or defeat of the Industrial University. Two other letters whooping it up for Turner's Plan appeared in this number, and best of all, a signed editorial from Wright urging the State Legislature to consider Turner's project deeply and to finance it not with College and Seminary funds but with the "Swamp Lands" grant which Congress had given the State at the time of the Illinois Central grant but which had been generally forgotten.

Buoyant, Kennicott went to Springfield that June to serve as President of the Industrial College Convention and to shape its action even more solidly toward Wright's idea of financing. Publishing the Convention's actions in

(2) Semi-centennial History of the University of Illinois, by Burt E. Powell, 1918, Vol. 1, p. 25.

the August issue, he was rewarded by reading in the September number Wright's explanation of his course in the whole matter. Up to now, said Wright, he had kept quiet, hoping that his objections to Turner's Plan would be thrashed out in controversy. He approved its main purpose, but he hadn't liked to think about farmers receiving education by themselves, and he certainly opposed the use of the Seminary and College Funds for the training of farmers and mechanics exclusively. But now, from the proceedings of the Springfield Convention, he was happy to learn he had been in error, "the whole plan being to provide good teachers and by-and-by as funds can be produced and advancements safely made, to provide means of instruction of the highest order. . . . It would at once be seen that to establish a Normal School or Teacher's Seminary with less classical and more practical instruction would be right and proper . . . and the addition of a professorship of practical agriculture and one or more of mechanics . . . would give in full the Agricultural College or Industrial University of Professor Turner."

He rejoiced that "all our plans harmonize so entirely" and urged his readers to "see if the next Legislature cannot be made to do its duty." He annexed a petition for signers, and concluded "Let it be well circulated!"

That done, he turned quickly and persuaded Dr. Kennicott to take the post of horticultural and educational editor of *The Prairie Farmer*.

"John S. Wright has sucked me in," Kennicott wrote Turner on October 27. "He is to pay me $25 per month . . ."

To Wright, this grip on "The Old Doctor" was fortunate. It would give the paper new authority in horticultural matters, and appease the Turner forces. It would also allow him to set sail for England with certainty that the paper would not suffer. Privately he felt sure Ambrose Wight would soon return to the editorship, for *The Herald of the Prairies* was obviously failing.

Ambrose Wight was, indeed, ready to return by December 8, for on that date Kennicott, in dismay, learned that the man he disliked was returning as part owner and "sole editor." From England Wright made the arrangements and the January, 1853, issue appeared as "Edited by J. Ambrose Wight; John S. Wright and J. Ambrose Wight Proprietors, 171 Lake Street, Chicago." Luther Haven disappeared in the reshuffling.

"I know that John S. Wright is measurably with us," Kennicott wrote Turner, "but I fear Mr. Wight will temporize and let our articles be misprinted in his paper."

Except for a few months in late 1854 and early in 1855, Kennicott remained as Horticultural Editor as long as John S. Wright published the paper. Each month he filled from four to six pages with his pomological news and his appeals to the settlers to raise more fruit.

"We have good peach land and plenty of it, and fortunes will one day be made by raising peaches in Illinois," particularly Southern Illinois, he kept predicting.

Constantly exploring the practical as well as the scientific in his zeal to help the prairie people, he introduced if indeed he did not invent, "The Baby Jumper" which, by suspending a baby in a combination cloth bucket and saddle at the end of a long pole fastened between logs in a cabin wall, allowed the infant to bounce up and down most happily while its mother turned to other duties.

Seen first by *The Prairie Farmer* at Kennicott's home it was described in the August, 1846, issue, as an invention of great importance. It grew to national proportions within six years and was sold in various patent forms without any recognition of "The Old Doctor's" part in its history.

Only Professor Turner was more influential than Kennicott in the long and bitter fight with clerical-professors and Illinois college presidents over the proposed diversion of governmental funds to a new non-sectarian university. He was one of the leaders in The Industrial League which drove Turner's "Plan" forward, and in the endless conventions and mass-meetings which preached the cause, he was either on the floor or in the chair much of the time.

From John S. Wright, a decade before, he had learned the trick of having school conventions coincide with agricultural meetings, and since he was active in farm bodies, it was easy for him to manage well.

When the Illinois Legislature on February 9, 1853, passed a bill urging the Federal Congress to grant land for the system of State Universities, "The Old Doctor" was in the lobbies, coaxing, threatening, pushing the cause forward. And, like his fellow workers, he felt that Illinois should have the credit for initiating the movement when, in 1857, the agitation had grown so general that a Vermont Senator, Justin B. Morrill, introduced in Congress a bill embodying the demands. Passing in 1862, the bill was signed by President Lincoln on July 2, and the States were at last assured of universities where the higher education should be free, practical and non-sectarian.

On that date John S. Wright might well have recalled how this same Lincoln, as a Legislator in a near-bankrupt State, had aided his first crusade for better teachers for lonely children on the swampy frontier.

"The Old Doctor" lived to see the Land Grant Bill win, but by the following spring he was failing even as the blossoms were falling from his acres of fruit trees—trees that he loved like sons. There were blossoms of all known prairie flowers and exotics, too, in his long beds of black Illinois loam when, on June 4, 1863, he died. It was his old adversary, J. Ambrose Wight who wrote the dead man's best epitaph: "He was a peculiar man . . . transparent as a child. . . . More than any man in the Northwest, he gave himself to the public."

CHAPTER XIV

Rise and Fall of "The Human Arm"

D URING the long, lean years between his bankruptcy and his recovery, Wright had always told himself that never again would he make the mistake he had made in 1836 when he lost his real estate fortune by tying it up to a "safe, sound business." If he had had the courage of his own, wild, visionary convictions he would have ridden out that storm, rich and happy.

And always he had told himself that when real estate should made him rich again, he would return to his true course—live off the increasing yield as Chicago grew, and spend the excess rentals in the cause of education.

Now in 1851 he had arrived at that point. As in 1837, he had blocks of real estate and a warehouse. But now, in addition, he had income and a paper which, even if it produced no great profit, gave him vastly more in the way of influence and prestige. The time had come to sit back and think wholly about the subject that was so sacred to his mother: "I was satisfied with the property," he said, "wanted no more . . . being satisfied with what I had done and knowing that a few years would make it a fortune large enough for me and my family. . . . But I wanted more income, not in anything speculative but in a regular staid business."(¹)

His father had insisted upon just this step in 1836; in 1851 it was Wright's own idea.

It was the agricultural implement business that lured

(1) Chicago: Past, Present, Future, by John S. Wright, 1870.

him. As early as 1841 he had been interested in farm implements, not as a manufacturer, but as a tester. He had brought samples of new machines to the "repository" of the Union Agricultural Society in Chicago, and had had farmers try them in the fields. He had seen to it that the early Union Agricultural Society Fairs stressed, in their premium list, farm machinery, particularly the plow. Next to a hedge fence, the most pressing need of the settlers in the late 1830s and the 1840s was a plow that would cut the wild grass and its prodigious roots. Plows, brought from the East, had been, in Ambrose Wight's opinion, "little better than the hooked sticks of the Egyptians" when it came to turning the sod, and *The Prairie Farmer* had encouraged inventors to produce "the Western plow"—an

Seed sower. An optimistic advertisement printed in *The Prairie Farmer*, July 22, 1858, when the rage for labor-saving machinery was so strong in the west.

implement of steel whose polished surface would not clog
and scratch as would the old ones of wrought iron. By
1846 a half-dozen plow-makers were busy within the ter-
ritorial bounds of the Union Agricultural Society, and the
paper was noting that John Lane in Will county, had been
making them in 1842. John Deere, a blacksmith of Grand
Detour had used an old sawmill steel blade in making his
plow as early as 1837 and by 1846 had been producing a
thousand plows a year. The next year he moved to Moline
where, in 1851, he was selling 4,000 a year and many seed-
drills, too.

Toward the reaper there had been less interest. As
early as 1824 "Harvey's Great Amazement," the invention
of a New York State boy, Harvey May, had cut wheat
well, but had perished because neighbors laughed and
Harvey's father had told him "patent laws only drew men
into ruinous lawsuits."(2) The West had been cool toward

(2) *The Prairie Farmer*, October, 1854.

"The Soldier's Great Benefactor." By such advertisements as this,
manufacturers of farm machinery pushed sales during the Civil War.
From *The Prairie Farmer*, December 26, 1863.

The first picture of McCormick's "Virginia Reaper" to be published in *The Prairie Farmer*, December, 1846.

stories of McCormick's reaper in Virginia and Hussey's in Maryland up to the hour when the Mexican War had taken so many strong-armed wheat cradlers from the fields, forecasting, incidentally, the greater need that would come during the Civil War.

McCormick had sold a few of his machines as far west as Missouri in 1844 and in 1845, George Esterly, a farmer at Heart Prairie, Wisconsin, produced a machine which, when pushed by two horses, cut the heads from a promised 20 acres a day. One farmer wrote Wright's paper that this machine "can cut a field all to destructive smash. . . . It walks over the ground like an elephant."

One of the proprietors of the McCormick "Virginia Reaper" called at *The Prairie Farmer* office in September, 1845, saying he was "endeavoring to introduce the machines in the West" at $120 each. He guaranteed it would cut an acre and a half in an hour and save a bushel an acre now lost in "ordinary cradling." Farmers, reading this, made comparisons: One man to drive, one to rake the cut wheat off the platform, five men to bind the sheaves. Thus, seven men and three horses could harvest 12 to 14 acres a day. In cutting wheat by hand, seven cradlers followed by seven rakers and binders and three shockers might cut 20 acres a day.

Each man working with the binder would be good for two acres a day, each man on the cradling crew for less than one and one-fifth.

Many inventors, as rapidly as their patents had been applied for, licensed blacksmiths and mechanics to manufacture their machines in their several localities. This sale of "patent rights" at high figures violated the sentiments of the average Western settler who argued that in a democracy inventions of public use should be available at low cost to the actual producers. Still, the hunger for the machines was so great that settlers of a mechanical turn of mind took leases for local territories and mortgaged their farms to buy iron and hire workmen.

"It walks over the ground like an elephant." Esterly's Harvester. From *The Prairie Farmer*, December, 1846.

Lavishing columns of type and wood-cut illustrations upon the reapers, encouraging their general adoption, and predicting their eventual displacement of the cradle everywhere, Wright's paper, nevertheless, in September, 1846, trying to halt the rush toward the "homemade" machines, warned its readers:

"The farmer is not generally a mechanic, and where he has been at a great expense for a machine that will not go, he is not in a condition to remedy the evil. And though in cases he is ready to curse the knavery of the man who traded him his patent, he ought rather to curse his own greenness. . . . If the farmer will resolve to see his implement *work* before he buys it, and then buy the *machine* instead of the *right to build it*, he will save himself some wasted temper, as well as coppers."

But the mania for inventing reapers rose till in 1849 the editors reported "a multitude of different patterns with different names." Manufacturers wooed John S. Wright's favor, for publicity about their machines in the West's most powerful farm paper was extremely valuable. They tempted Ambrose Wight to come out to the fields and compare their machines with their rivals', and then if his report—and his reprint of what the farmers said about the machines—failed to be enthusiastic enough, they wrote furious letters to the paper. They took advertisements in the paper giving testimonials from happy users, bitter denunciations of other reapers, and demands for the correction of unwarranted slights.

In November, 1849, J. Haines drove his invention, a new reaper, long miles from Whiteside county into Chicago, so that he could put it through its clanking evolu-

Hussey's Reaper and Mower. From *The Prairie Farmer*, May, 1852.

tions, mowing imaginary grain, up and down Lake Street outside *The Prairie Farmer* office windows.

Inventors from Illinois, Wisconsin, Indiana, Michigan, crowded Wright's editorial door, describing machines with reels, machines without reels, machines that cut the grain with "a great number of sheep shears," machines whose cutting bars sliced off the stalks at the root, machines that contented themselves with the heads, and machines that did their own raking.

From the moment McCormick's and Hussey's reapers had arrived in the West there had been complaints about the difficulty of raking the cut wheat from the platform. Ambrose Wight, reporting his first view of McCormick's machine in operation, described the raking as done "by a short, rose-faced, muscular man who rode backwards astride a sort of rail, with a stout piece of board attached to keep him from falling off: His legs were so short that he could only touch one toe; and he hung thus in the air, doing his work much as a man lifts a basket over a fence across the top of which he lies balancing himself. If it is not hard work for him, it was hard work to look at him."

Here and there inventors brought out self-rakers to meet the demand. There was Foster's in 1846 and Andrew C. Cook's at Richmond, Indiana, in 1848. Cyrus McCormick, moving to Chicago in 1847 and going into partnership with C. M. Gray, the city's most famous cradle-maker, promised the public that his '47 machines, 500 in number, would rake much easier. He and the other established manufacturers derided the self-raking principle mercilessly.

But the pressure for it became greater, as indeed, for all kinds of reapers, in 1849 when the news of Captain Sutter's discovery of gold on the Pacific slope struck the West. In its July issue, *The Prairie Farmer* reminded settlers how deeply the Mexican War had cut into its supply of field hands:

"We apprehend it will be much more so now, in consequence of the immense drainage of laboring force for the golden war of California. Only those who live on the great thoroughfares have much idea of how universal this drainage is. Some of the New York papers have undertaken, from time to time, to give lists of the emigrants. They might as well undertake the census of a drove of mosquitoes. Every town and neighborhood in the West has sent somebody, and generally a troop, to people the Pacific region."

In this peril, the reaper was a "great redeeming influence. . . . Without this the harvests of the two past years would have gone, to some extent, ungathered; but the amount of it will be vastly increased the present season."

It estimated that each of the 2,800 reapers in use in the West would save, as claimed, "the labor of four and a half men." In addition there were 180 of Esterly's Harvesters, each saving the work of twenty men. "We count the work of the Reaper at twelve acres, and of a Harvester at sixteen acres." With the machines supplanting 30,000 men "we can see that the Northwestern states can spare a goodly force for the Californias, and yet get along with their work."

By 1851 Wright had convinced himself that the making of reapers was "the regular, staid business, not at all speculative" for which he was looking, and in November he went into partnership with Obed Hussey, expecting that Baltimorean to now do what the Virginian, McCormick, had done—move to Chicago where the arrival of several railroads was imminent and where by the end of the year three million bushels of wheat would arrive in Chicago from the Illinois and Michigan Canal, from wagons and from the new Galena and Chicago railway. But Hussey refused to move and Wright had to content himself with the mere right to manufacture the Hussey machine for seven midland States.

Building a factory, Wright added the patent corn plow of William Beard of Door Village, Indiana, to his work, and kept examining patents of various implements as he heard of them. He was in a hurry to find a reaper upon which he could lavish his creative ideas. By February of 1852 the Michigan Southern Railroad would reach Chicago and connect it with the East; by May the Michigan Central would reach town, and the Illinois Central would arrive with it. By 1854 the Chicago, Milwaukee & St. Paul would be due, also the Chicago, Rock Island and Pacific. What had once been merely one of "Wright's wild goose chases— one of his visionary schemes" was on the eve of reality— a reality sufficient to make Chicago the railroad center of the nation. Six railroads in six years, bringing immigrants to town so rapidly that the city was to jump from 38,733 in '52 to 60,662 in '54, an increase of some 60 per cent.

Wright in '51 saw what the combination of reapers and railroads would do for Chicago as a wheat market. Here the farmers would come with their grain and for their machines. The Soo canal at the northern end of Lake Michigan was to be opened by 1855 and would swell Chicago's importance as a port. Actually Chicago in 1853 would ship more than 6,000,000 bushels of grain, nearly 13,000,000 in '54, over 16,000,000 in '55, and lead Wright's pupil in "boosterism," William Bross, to exult in 1855, "Chicago is the greatest primary grain port in the world. Chicago's 13,000,000 in '54 stood compared with New York's 9,000,000, Archangel's 9,000,000, Odessa's 7,000,000. Bross crowed, that same year, that Illinois now had 2,410 miles of railroad track, and that Chicago was the center for 10 trunk lines and 11 branches, with 95 trains a day entering or leaving the city. "The world has never seen so much physical progress in so short a period."

Forseeing so much of this tremendous "boom" Wright,

in 1852, leaped at the news that a bed-ridden paralytic here in Chicago had produced an entirely new kind of reaper and was looking for someone to patent and finance it.

Investigating, he found that the man was Jearum Atkins, a Vermonter who as a boy had shamed all his teachers at mathematics whenever his poverty allowed him to get to school at all. At 15 he had learned the mill-wright's trade and had come, as a young man, to northern Illinois as an expert on water wheels for mills. Around 1841 a wagon loaded with milling machinery had upset on a steep hill and crippled him for life. Some ten years later, he was watching his savings slowly disappear while he fruitlessly tried to invent something in the few moments each day when he could sit up, the object of pity from the neighbors. One day a farmer, at his bedside, told him he could make his fortune if he could invent a mechanical rake for the reaper. Atkins had never seen one of the ma-chines, but he announced confidently, "I can do it." A neighbor wheeled a McCormick reaper in front of Atkins' window so that the invalid, properly propped up, could peep out at it as it went through its maneuvers. At the end of twenty minutes he had, as he later told it, grasped the whole thing. Immediately he set to work.

Desperately poor and dependent upon his friends and neighbors for support, he was given a drawing board suspended over his head, and on it, from his prostrate position, he began to work out the ideas that buzzed in his head. He kept saying, "If it will not work in my brain, it will not work anywhere" and for weeks together he was scarcely able to eat or sleep. With a rasp and file he made a model of a self-raking attachment, only to destroy it in disgust. Then he went to work on a wholly new principle— the imitation of the human arm. The rake would reach out, sweep the cut grain from the platform, draw back, then

Atkins "Automaton." From Wright's advertisement in *The Prairie Farmer*, June, 1853.

do it all over again. It was a most ingenious device and as the *Chicago Daily Ledger* later said, "it caught the ear, eye and more than that—the heart of John S. Wright . . . a citizen of Illinois who had done more than any one individual to elevate the standard of farming and horticulture in Illinois. We repeat it, *more than any one man.*"

A deal was soon made. Wright was to patent and introduce the machine as "Atkins' Automaton" and to own it half-and-half with Atkins. The patent applied for, Wright manufactured a sample in his factory, rushing it through so that it might be ready for the exhibition and trial of reapers at Geneva, New York, on July 20, 1852. Although some of the workmen fell ill, feverish night work had it finished by July 17, and next day it was shipped Eastward, having been seen but once by its inventor, Atkins. At the trial at Geneva, a rod broke and Wright lost the competition. However the machine was hailed by the Albany newspapers and workmen as "an extraordinary curiosity." Excited by the sensation he had caused, Wright sent the

Abraham Lincoln   Cyrus McCormick

Jonathan Turner   William Bross

machine to many other exhibitions and contests, winning first prize at the State Fairs of Ohio, Michigan and Wisconsin as well as at several county and agricultural society fairs. That winter of 1853 he built 40 for the coming harvest.

Cyrus McCormick, producing 1,500 for that season and as many if not more for the harvest of '54, derided self-rakers as "a new-fangled experiment" and in advertisements reminded farmers how often they had been humbugged by sensational new inventions in the past. But Wright, winning 42 first premiums at fairs in '53, made 300 machines for the '54 harvest, and 1,200 for 1855. McCormick, increasing to 2,650 for the '55 harvest, announced that in '56 he would produce 4,000. Wright announced he would raise to 3,000, and taunted McCormick's brother, William S., who was, at that time, writing the challenges and defiances in the war of words, "You have been twenty-two years in the business and have got up to 4,000 machines; I have been at it four years, and shall get out for next harvest at least 3,000 and shall try to come a little nearer to your number than that. Truly it does seem as though there was a good deal of reason for your fear of rivalry of this machine."

Even before Wright had become his rival, McCormick had complained that *The Prairie Farmer* had discriminated against him in its reports of the behavior of reapers in the field, and, according to Dr. Kennicott, McCormick had at one time gained "advantage to his interests" by threatening to start an opposition farm paper.[3] After the "Automaton" began its meteoric rise, McCormick's attacks became more bitter, and Wright replied in kind, both men inserting their arguments in the advertising columns of *The Prairie Farmer* and other Chicago newspapers, as well as in circulars.

(3) Kennicott to Turner, Turner Papers, Illinois State Historical Library.

When McCormick published claims that his machine could cut fifty per cent faster than the "Automaton," Wright offered to bet him $25,000 to $5,000 that it could not, and $3,000 to $1,000 that it couldn't beat the "Automaton" at all. He offered $5,000 to $1,000 that one man could work the "Automaton" through the whole competition with "greater ease than your driver and raker can do the work." He piled offer on offer as to details of the proposed trial and concluded, "Now, you braggart," here was a total of $98,000 against $30,000, and if Wright won, he'd give everything over the expenses of the competition, to the Illinois State Agricultural Society. He wouldn't specify how McCormick should spend any winnings. "Dispose of it as you please."

There was no acceptance. As a matter of fact both men had grown disgusted with the reaper trials which had become so popular an institution—festival days with crowds milling, cheering, groaning, betting, drinking as the rival machines raced through the grain. Unscrupulous manufacturers entered machines that had been secretly fortified, they bribed drivers and judges, and dosed horses with brandy. In time, the competitions, popularly called "flirts," passed into the realm of the fantastic, with contestants chaining their reapers together and then whipping horses to see which machine could pull the other apart.

Wright in 1854 came out against the system, saying that although he had won many of the events, he had felt in victory as he had felt in defeat that it was wholly unfair to require judges to decide between as many as twelve competitors in one afternoon's demonstration. He proposed, as a fairer test, one that would start in the South when the first wheat was ripe and progress Northward across the weeks, with all expenses, including the salaries of the judges, paid by the various State Agricultural Societies.

As he prepared for the 1856 season—the one in which he was to narrow the gap between his machine and Mc-Cormick's—Wright expanded triumphantly, paying $72,-000 for 52 acres on the North Branch of the Chicago River, using it as a site for an addition to his reaper factory, named "The Prairie Farmer Works." He arranged for the shipment of parts to branch offices in Dayton, Baltimore, Harrisburg and Rochester, N. Y., where the machines could be assembled, and repair work done. On July 1, an announcement for his August *Prairie Farmer* read:

"In these days of railroads, a monthly publication does not meet the public wants. From this point (Chicago), as the great commercial center of the northwest, railroads are soon to reach beyond the present outskirts of civilization, and there is no reason why the leading organ of the chief interests of this mighty region should not keep progress with the times. . . . Therefore The Prairie Farmer must be printed weekly."

The change would come next January when Ambrose Wight was to retire, and become an ordained minister, laboring in the slums of the booming city.

Crime and poverty were keeping step with the rise of Chicago. Fifty-seven hotels now burst with guests as Chicago became "the convention city." Its real estate was in '56 three times its '52 value. When business interests, that summer of '56, demanded that old Fort Dearborn's blockhouse and sagging oak stockade make way for progress, it was John S. Wright who, lovingly, bought it, and the following year imported special machinery for turning it into souvenir furniture for himself and his friends.(4)

Ambrose Wight grew eloquent about Western prosperity when he wrote, for the December issue, his last farewell. He recalled how the prairies had been sunk in

(4) The First Presbyterian Church, by P. A. Otis, 1900.

distrust and despair when he had come to the paper in
1843, and now, in 1855, there was money everywhere, railroads, "hedges such as no other part of the world can
boast of . . . prices such as make every farmer laugh in
his sleep whenever a breath of wind comes over his fields
to his bedchamber." He hated to quit. He bowed low to
John S. Wright as one who "has sustained The Prairie
Farmer for many years without other than a conscious-
ness of serving the public."

Wright gave his departing friend high praise, particularly for his diligence in protecting the readers "against
imposition and humbuggery." In his place was to reign
a triumvirate, Dr. Kennicott, Charles D. Bragdon, late of
Richland, N. Y., and Charles Betts, former editor of the
Michigan Farmer. Kennicott was to handle educational
news, since the reaper had made Wright "despair" of
handling schools properly himself any longer. The weekly
issue was to sell at $2 instead of $1. He expected the
monthly circulation of 8,900 to double, at least.

Forgotten, or at least postponed, was his vow to devote
his wealth to schools. His mother's voice was no longer
in his ear. She had died in April, 1854.

"We are wedded to no isms, influenced by no party,
directed by no personal interest, not even the love of
money," Wright announced in the first weekly issue, January, 1856. He gave the printing to the Chicago Tribune
Steam Printing Job Office, operated by Wright, Medill,
Day & Co.—the "Wright" being his brother, Timothy.

Dreams grew out of dreams. When the winter's ice
locked the lakes two weeks early, that winter of 1855-56,
cutting off two cargoes of seasoned wood for the '56 reapers, Wright sweepingly ordered Indiana and Michigan saw-
mills to rush new timber to him. He built "super-heated,
steam kiln-dryers" to dry this green wood quickly. Then
buoyantly, he struck off in March for the East, entrusting

the crucial factory work to a subordinate whom he later decided had been "an energetic, driving man, but utterly unfitted to direct a large business." What it was that called him away, he never said, merely declaring that "he had been obliged to go." (5)

In his absence, improperly dried wood went into the reapers and, in the hot sun of the extraordinarily dry, torrid summer of '56, the new Automatons warped, cracked, popped! "It was universal failure," Wright later said. "Payments had to be put over and a cash outlay (in repairs) incurred of $40 to $50 on each machine." At the time, however, he saw no permanent damage to his machine's reputation, and made even larger plans for the season of '57.

He pooh-poohed whispers from the East that another panic was impending. The Crimean War which had, through English purchases, taken vast quantities of salted beef from Chicago in 1855, ended in February, 1856, and orders had consequently dropped like a plummet. To Wright it was incredible that the end of a foreign war could mean anything drastic to so rapidly growing and so rich a nation as the United States. He reasoned that all these armies of immigrants pouring in from Europe would mean ever-increasing wealth for the nation. There was a natural reaction, he realized, from the fever of railroad speculation and the issuance of so many reckless bank notes in the West. But all that was trivial—the land was rich, the people were coming, Chicago was the capital of a region that could produce prodigiously, good times or bad.

Writing a new circular for 1857 he published testimonials from farmers who showed "stronger confidence than ever before" in the Automaton. He refused to heed a growing murmur of criticism that the "human arm" got out of fix too often.

(5) "Chicago: Past, Present, Future," by John S. Wright, 1870, p. 295n.

But by March, 1857, when some Illinois banks failed, there came a sign that Wright was worried. In that month's issue of his paper, one of the editors wrote a long tribute to the Automaton, declaring that in so doing he was acting without Wright's consent or knowledge. The significance of this move lay in the fact that only as recently as January, 1856, Wright had told his readers that he never had and never would use *The Prairie Farmer* to advance his private interests. Several rival machines had received more notice in its columns than had the Automaton. Indeed, he had never asked Ambrose Wight to mention it, "and it was more than two years after I had engaged in the business before he had seen one of the machines or penciled a line concerning it." Automaton salesmen had complained about Wright's excess of scruples.

Now in '57 Wright's proud editorial position was lost.

In June he penned a furious editorial against Easterners who spread wild alarms about the financial collapse of the West—they were only trying to frighten their neighbors from emigrating to the great new country. Look at the facts about emigration! Each railroad to the West was running from three to five trains a day often so large as to necessitate two engines "while those to the East of the first class are not half-filled and of the second class and emigrant nearly empty. Our accession is counted by hundreds and thousands annually. . . . Never before were so many coming West."

He admitted there had been wild, foolish speculation at some points in the West, particularly as to town sites, "yet at some of these wilderness points there will be during the lifetime of many men now in active life, cities springing into existence that shall outnumber all the cities of the Atlantic States, not ten of them excepted. This is the destiny of the West. All the prating about folly and extravagance—all the warning of ruin to come—cannot stop the human currents flowing hitherward and which insures a degree of prosperity certain as that of the past."

And in his July 2 issue he reprinted with eagerness the *Philadelphia News Letter's* description of the tremendous flow of immigration to the West from the Atlantic seaboard as the true cause of the depression. "A million emigrants each taking $100 on the average will go west in 1857," said the Philadelphia editor. "It is the infusion of this mighty stream of gold into the currency of the West that has so quickened it into activity and the abstraction of it from the currency of the East that has given an alarming sluggishness to trade."

Seven days after Wright published this cheering news, the Bank of Commerce in Chicago blew, and by the middle of July Illinois knew that the drouth and the blistering heat would cut the farm crops most seriously. By late July, newspapers were calling the crops "a total failure," and by September 30, Deacon Bross' *Democratic Press* was saying the national panic "has no parallel in our business history." Wright held on, preaching as he had exactly twenty years before, that Chicago and the West were even surer of their destiny than ever. But the farmers couldn't pay for their reapers—nor for *The Prairie Farmer*. Correspondence, the thing that had built the paper, had fallen off in 1856 and '57. Bragdon and Betts wrote with an edge of sarcasm, a straining for "brightness" that antagonized the readers. To crowd down the live, lean arguments and experiences of practical farmers, the new editors had pushed in columns of trashy fiction, feeble discussions of manners, and an affected and witless children's "corner."

In March Wright had issued an appeal for subscribers to pay up. He, who had at fifteen been a prodigy at keeping books in his father's store, now at 43 confessed that he

didn't know whether it was $10,000 or $15,000 now owed
by delinquent subscribers. He did know there had been
a deficit of $4,000 in '56. An advertising and business mana-
ger, Robert Cox, was brought on from Washington, D. C.,
to try and straighten out the paper's finances, and in the
September 10 issue, the sheet's commercial reporter wrote
that Chicago's "financial status has been and still is un-
shaken" amid all the hard times that had beset the gamblers in stocks and bonds on Wall Street.

But when advertising which had stood at ten columns
in January, 1856, fell to one column on September 24, 1857,
Wright gave up, and handed the paper to his printers,
James C. and William H. Medill. He had not time to note
how, two days before, there had been laid at Bloomington
the cornerstone of the State Normal School which had
been conceived in his heart.

The circle was complete. The panic of '37 had brought
him the paper, the panic of '57 was taking it away.

Wright let it go, and after it, his real estate, piece by
piece, in an effort to save the "Automaton." Little by little
all those blocks and acres that had so recently been worth
$600,000 and a comfortable income each year—all went.
And, what was worse for Wright, his wife's property went,
too. It had been settled upon her in flush times, but he had
continually used it as collateral for loans without security
to her, so confident was he of the future. Then as he later
put it, "When my reverses came in 1857, not expecting to
be seriously embarrassed, and fearing that my property
would be tied up with judgments, all was assigned to
secure endorsers."

It was to his brothers, who had endorsed some of
his notes, that he assigned much of his property. He
didn't blame them for demanding it. They were, he said,
"heavily involved" and "under the pressure of the times";
under the same circumstances "most persons would have

endeavored as they did to take care of themselves."

Uncomplaining, save to blame himself for not having remembered his '37 lesson about trusting to real estate speculation instead of some "staid business," Wright found himself back where he had been twenty years before—fortune gone, his glorious city in despair and poverty, men mocking him with his own soaring predictions of the past, his wife bitterly disillusioned as to her children's future, and completely vindicated in all the scornful things she had said about Chicago.

But Wright merely picked up his pen and began writing another circular—commencing, "The money panic has brought a most favorable time to buy Chicago property—."

In the excitement over patent mechanisms, this complicated and fantastic apple peeler was advertised in *The Prairie Farmer*, June, 1853.

CHAPTER XV

The Bird in the Red Sky

IT WAS not until the convulsions of the Civil War had struck the nation that Wright gave up hope of reviving the "Atkins Automaton." From 1858 to 1861 he planned and schemed while across Western fields the reaper business kept on garnering fortunes for those manufacturers who could still extend credit.

From somewhere, perhaps from his brothers, perhaps from some pittance saved from his own wreckage, Wright was able to hold his family together and maintain an office. In between his efforts to recover his reaper, he caught gleams of another fortune in real estate. As in the late 1840s, it was vividly apparent to him that hard times offered wise investors their greatest opportunities, but as in that earlier time, he found Eastern capitalists groaning over their folly in ever having touched property in Chicago.

Even those who had followed his advice and financed the Western railroads or bought land which those railroads rocketed upward in value, forgot the profits they had made, and saw only the current deflation. He had often pointed out that Chicago, more than any other city in the nation, had been built by outside capital. It had been Eastern money that had done it, and Wright had done more than any other one man to start it coming.

But now he found that his very prominence as a manufacturer, a wealthy landowner and preacher of future glories had only dramatized his own failure; it was not as a boy but as a prominent man that he had fallen this time.

194

A circular written by him in '58 to persuade bargain hunters to make him their agent, never saw daylight.

Undismayed by so many cold shoulders, he wrote a new circular in March, 1860, proposing the organization of two joint-stock companies and taking as his keynote: "The depression exists and those who are wise will avail themselves of it. With even more pertinacity than from 1846 to 1850—more confidence in the wisdom of the advice—would I urge you not to let this golden opportunity slip."

Less than a half dozen copies of this pamphlet had been mailed when lawyers told him he was in no position to act as agent for purchasers; the plan would make him personally liable. So he scrapped it and incorporated "The Land Investment Company" to deal in Chicago real estate with himself as manager. It was, however, February 22, 1861, before the Legislature gave him his incorporation papers, and the Civil War was looming; secession of the Cotton States was shattering the confidence of all financiers. To him it was perfectly plain that the war would not only fail to harm Chicago's growth but that it would increase it immeasurably. "No earthly power," he wrote in a new circular, "not even the dissolution of the Union, can divert from Chicago the business and the traffic of the great Northwest."

The crisis sharpened his mind almost to the point of clairvoyance. While the whole North rang with the cry that the war would be over in ninety days, sixty days, Wright in his circular said that the North underestimated entirely the endurance and independence of the South. Statesmen and militarists were announcing that the naval blockade would quickly strangle the Confederacy, but Wright dissented. He wrote that the Southerners would raise corn and wheat in place of cotton. "Of course, comforts and luxuries from abroad, and even many necessities, are to be dispensed with, but in that they glory. No doubt, for a year or two, or longer, the South will live very well within themselves."

While Southerners bragged that each of them could whip from five to twenty Yankees, Wright declared "It will take a year or two of fighting to teach them proper respect for Northern courage." Wholly unversed in military affairs, he put his finger on the South's true course, long before it had been shaped; "The conflict on the part of the South will be mainly defensive, which gives them greatly the advantage." Without knowing it, he was arriving at the viewpoint of most professional military experts in Europe, who agreed that the South, fighting defensively on interior lines, had much the better chance of success.

Since his circular of 1861 was never circulated, there were no voices raised, later in the war, to point out how accurate had been his forecast as to the length of the war, and the slowness with which the blockade could take effect. In 1863 and '64 there was so much grain ripening and stored out across the bulk of the Confederacy that invading Union armies marvelled, and often left their own supplies in boxes, living fatly off the country. And it was the opinion of military experts, after the war, that the South might well have triumphed had it remained on the defensive and not wasted its precious man-power in offensive excursions into Maryland, Kentucky, Missouri and Pennsylvania.

To Wright there could be no question but that the war would be waged for years in the Border States, and that this would mean a vast diversion of trade from Cincinnati and St. Louis to Chicago. Common sense decreed this shift of business from danger to safety. In 1847 he had been ridiculed for saying that Chicago, with one-third of Cincinnati's population, would overtake its rival within 15 years. Now in 1861 this was as good as accomplished. In

1848 he had said that Chicago would surpass St. Louis, too, but so many of his own fellow-Chicagoans had declared it "visionary even to suppose we could rival her" that he had restrained himself on the subject in his writings. But by 1858 his study of the railroads in their relation to agriculture and population, so emboldened him that he signed the prediction: Chicago would soon outdo the great Queen City of the River. Now in 1861 it had practically pulled abreast of St. Louis and everybody saw that the race was as good as over.

Back in 1837 he had made Pittsburghers' jaws drop by telling them that the mud trading-post Chicago would, in the near future, dwarf their city. In less than a decade it had been done. In his '61 pamphlet he threw open the throttle and went the whole hog, announcing that his city would surpass Philadelphia before 1900. When he repeated this prediction on the street, mocking laughter was the only response, for Philadelphia had been the second city for so long that its position seemed secure. It was five times the size of Chicago! Yet by 1890 his prediction had come true.

In '61 he predicted that within "twenty or thirty years" Chicago would be twice the size of St. Louis. Within twenty-five years it had come true.

As if the strain of all these brilliant forecasts had been too much for him, Wright erratically threw down his pen while correcting the proofs of this '61 pamphlet and rushed to New York to secure the advice of James T. Soutter, who, as the former head of the Bank of the Republic, had what Wright knew to be "unbounded influence upon capitalists." Soutter, however, pleaded ill-health. He was just leaving for Europe. Strangely Wright decided to await his return, and sat in New York for almost three years!

Meanwhile, just as he had said it would, Chicago blossomed and burgeoned as the war-born trade rushed to it and opportunities for his own particular kind of activity begged to be handled. McCormick's reaper, doing the work of the missing farm boys, was credited by members of Lincoln's Cabinet with having done more for the Union cause than any general. But Wright stayed far from his beloved city in the period of its greatest "boom" and even let the printer, back there, break up the type for the '61 circular so that, except for a few proofs, there remained nothing to prove what prophecies it had contained.

Just as Wright saw the future more clearly now than ever before, he was also seeing the present less clearly. Many forces were tearing at him. His wife was violently pro-Southern and grew naturally more violent as she heard the soldiers, marching through Chicago, chant with almost a religious roll their paean to "John Brown's Body" —that "evil" old man who had "murdered" her brother. Three of her nephews, sons of her sister 'Tina, who had married Dr. Lewis O'Connor Cordell of Charlestown, Virginia, had gone into the Confederate army. The husband of Wright's sister, Anne, Joseph Dana Webster, left his Chicago business for a war career that would make him a general close to Ulysses S. Grant. Wright's friends, notably Senator Stephen A. Douglas, Judge Caton and William Bross were beating the drums for Lincoln's cause.

Never having been able to share the anti-slavery passions of his fellow-reformers from New England, Wright found himself unable to adopt their zeal for the war. His own closeness to agriculture made him shrink from endorsing a conflict between the farmers of the Upper and the Lower Mississippi Valley. His own prophecy that the Illinois Central Railroad and intersectional commerce would make the Union indissoluble haunted him. Into his '61 circular he put a scorching denunciation of "the selfish, fiery zealots of South Carolina" and the "equally wicked, foolish, Northern Abolitionists." War was being made by "conspirators and fanatics."

Shortly before the outbreak of the war, his eleven-year-old daughter, Maria, had gone from Chicago to Virginia with one of his wife's relatives who had been West on a visit, and when the fighting began, his wife had made her way through the lines to reach the child. Kitty's difficulties were so great that she decided not to risk bringing Maria back with her and so returned to Chicago alone. Maria would be safe with relatives and, besides, everybody in Virginia was saying that the chivalry of the South would quickly carry the war into the North, and force the Lincoln Administration to its knees. Richmond was sure to be the safest of places!

Meanwhile Wright sat in New York waiting for Soutter to come back from Europe. On the streets, in the offices, in the newspapers raged the debate as to whether a State had the legal right to secede and whether the Federal Power had the right to coerce a State into remaining within the Union. Wright thought and thought about the puzzling question. Soon he was in libraries, digging into dusty tomes. Reading the files of the *Federalist* and the papers of James Madison, he concluded that Madison had failed to understand where the real sovereignty in the nation lay. This led him into wider and deeper research which convinced him that not only the Founding Fathers but practically every historian who had written about the subject had gone astray.

"We are in civil war from confusion of theories," he said, and took up the study of foreign authorities, Hooker, Grotius, Vattel, Pufendorf, Aristotle and the Old Testament. It had been thirty years, at least, since as a child-prodigy he had mastered dead languages, and he now found that he needed help in probing into Greek and Latin. From the little he could make out, with his rusty memory of those tongues, and from his comparison of the originals with existing translations, he felt sure that the scholars who had done the translating "had not altogether apprehended the writers of the free States of antiquity upon Government and history."

What was needed was a scholar to make wholly new translations for him, and he took his problem to his friend Professor S. F. B. Morse whom he had treated seriously years before when Morse was being laughed at for experimenting with a thing called the telegraph. For some months Morse had been giving Wright's project what Wright took to be serious encouragement, and now Morse recommended a preacher, J. Holmes Agnew, a specialist in dead languages, to be the translator.

By the beginning of 1863 Wright had spent almost two years on his quest, but he felt that his discoveries if perfected might stop the war. Friends in Chicago and New York agreed to help finance his research in part, at least. And the exclamations of excitement from his preacher-assistant, as the translations progressed, stirred him all the more. The Reverend Agnew not only announced that his employer had been amply justified in suspecting that previous translators had missed the meat of the ancient texts, but that what was needed was brand new translations to be published entire. Agnew announced that as soon as his work for Wright was done he would issue these volumes himself. Wright, whipped up to new enthusiasm by all this, decided that his own work on sovereignty would come out in five volumes, each containing from 500 to 550 pages.

Like a man possessed, he toiled in the bowels of libraries week in, week out, while the war went on. It came closer to him in the summer of 1863 when his daughter Maria was brought through the lines under a flag of truce. The child's experiences in the supposedly secure city of Richmond had been strenuous.

During the Seven Days Battle of 1862 when the Yankees had hammered up to the very gates of the city, she had stood on the sidewalks, under a blazing sun, to hold umbrellas over wounded Confederates, fan groaning men and give water to the dying. She had seen Stonewall Jackson's body lying in state in Richmond. Her relatives had been kindness itself but food had grown short in 1863 and they had sent her North under a flag of truce. The transfer was made at the depot for exchanging prisoners and a Confederate general (She thought it was John Macgruder), laughed as he handed her over, saying "Here's a little Reb for you." As the Confederate boat pulled away with both sides hurrahing for their leaders, little Maria had jumped to her feet, among the blue-coats, and had cheered for "Jeff Davis and the Southern Confederacy." The woman who was caring for her pulled at her dress, frightened, but the Yankee officers entertained her in their cabins, had her sing Rebel songs and escorted her gallantly to the home of family friends in Baltimore where her father was awaiting her.

He took her with him to New York and put her in the Misses Howland's school, which she remembered later as "expensive and exclusive." Wright was getting funds from somewhere for his research and Professor Morse was financing the publication of an introductory pamphlet which Wright had prepared to send forth as a sample of the five massive volumes to come. In January, 1864, he wrote this, the largest of all his circulars, calling it "Citizenship, Sovereignty, Published for American Citizens, The True Maintainers of State Sovereignty." For short, he called it "The Compend," and filled the fly leaves with suggestions that readers buy it at $5 a dozen to give neighbors or to send to soldiers in the field.

Among the testimonials contained in the fly-leaves was one from Professor Morse, revealing that while he couldn't

subscribe to everything Wright had advanced in the book,
and he certainly differed with Wright on the nature of
sovereignty, he thought no intelligent man should be without a copy. He concluded, "Gladly would I give you further
pecuniary help to bring out your larger work, but I have
so many calls from other sources that I can not."

Readers—and there were never many—found the Compend a perplexing jumble of long quotations from ancient
authorities, misty generalizations, and labored arguments
which only served to increase the mystery as to where
sovereignty really lay. As near as a reader could tell, the
South had been wrong in seceding and the North wrong
in denying it the right to secede. It argued that the war
should end with both the Union and slavery restored and
with the farming "Aristocracy" overthrowing the newly
risen class of Northern "harpies, scavengers, vile cheats
who have been plundering public coffers." It denounced
the new-rich war profiteers who "want to change our form
of government and introduce a Nobility with its rights of
primogeniture and entail."

Lincoln was, to Wright, merely "one of the most honest
straightforward patriots ever in the Executive chair" who
had "in his inexperience and bewilderment" been led by
"fanatical partisans and greedy spoil hunters" into such
unconstitutional excesses as the blockade of ports, the un-
authorized increase in the army and navy, the illegal ar-
rest of citizens, the suppression of the writ of habeas
corpus, his interference with the press and other acts
which constituted "the most infamous, outrageous usur-
pations of modern days." He felt sure Lincoln, when
given opportunity to study international principles, would
confess his errors and promptly guard against any other
President ever following his "dangerous precedents."

His old professor, Mark Hopkins, who was now president of Williams College looked the Compend over and

wrote him that it "was the most wonderful gathering of the great ideas of the world upon the depth of politics." But the pamphlet was a total failure. It neither sold, itself, nor inspired any person to come forth with offers to help finance the publication of the five volumes which it advertised. This meant that Wright had touched bottom as a pamphleteer. Of his last four, three had failed to be printed at all, and the fourth was being ignored.

Some consolation remained for Wright in the prominence the *New York Evening Post* in January, 1862, gave his letter describing a method by which the Government could sell its bonds at reduced interest after the war—a proposal which was ignored but which was remembered long afterwards when Federal bonds did sell at three per cent interest.

His Compend dying on the vine, Wright came home to a Chicago that had vastly changed. He was no longer one of the prominent citizens. The streets and offices and lobbies were full of jostling, blatant newcomers who had never heard of him. He played chess with Hiram Kennicott and spent weeks, either with or without his wife, at Hiram's "Folly". His elder son, Augustine, with something of his father's boyhood precocity, was learning civil engineering on the Union Pacific Railroad as it inched Westward. His daughter Maria was sent to Vassar.

By 1867 the tempo of the town got into his veins once more and with a rush he obtained options to buy $2,000,000 worth of property in a belt running entirely around the city. He sat down to write a circular which would, he felt certain, persuade Eastern capitalists to provide the two million and give him his chance, as promoter and manager, to make a fortune. As he wrote, his imagination winged into the future, and the more he showed that the shape of things to come lay in the mirror of the past, the more the past came crowding in and soon he found that he was

writing as much a history of Chicago as a prospectus of
its future. Chicago and St. Louis newspapers had been
exchanging brags and jeers and, having clipped the live-
liest of these, Wright decided to incorporate them, with
his own personal comments, in the volume.

"Chicago: Past, Present and Future Relations to the
Great Interior and to the Continent" he called it as, in
1868, it came from press, 404 pages long. Like "Citizenship, Sovereignty" it jumbled together important fact,
imaginative flights, dull statistics, vivid memories of
Chicago's history, and extraneous harangues, but it was
preserved from its predecessor's fate by the very presence
of the author's own reminiscences cropping out here and
there in unexpected places.

In it lay the evidence of how remarkable had been his
prophecies about Chicago, but few readers cared to wade
through shoals of figures to discover this. Nevertheless, the
book, for all its faults, was a tremendous hymn to a city,
and the newspapers and business interests of Chicago
praised it fulsomely. Understanding that the Board of
Trade had made "a positive engagement to take at least
1,362 copies" of a second edition, he published it only to
find that the Board of Trade hadn't so understood it, or
had backed out of the agreement. Disappointment again!

His second son, Chester, joined Augustine in railroad engineering, this time in Missouri, his wife returned to Virginia for a prolonged visit, and he and Maria found sanctuary under the "Folly's" roof where Hiram Kennicott
sat with open arms.

"Next to coming to Chicago," Wright wrote his sons
on October 20, 1870, "the best thing your mother can do
for the credit of her family is to go to her boys and stay
with them while they are there. This breaking up is perfectly shameful."

In the spring and summer of 1871 Wright penned two

more circulars proposing the purchase of between 2,000 and 4,500 acres, which he held on option, between Washington Heights and Blue Island on the city's outskirts. When it should be sold at a fabulous profit, the capitalists were supposed to pocket one-half, Wright and his sub-agents a quarter, while the remaining one-fourth was to go to schools and churches.

In August he was summoned to Mexico, Missouri, to bring back Maria who had come down with typhoid fever while visiting her brothers, and in October she was still bedfast in the home of his friend Dr. George E. Shipman on North Peoria Street in Chicago. With his wife gone again on a visit out of town, Wright slept in a room adjoining his office on East Washington Street, and he was there the night of October 8, 1871, when a knock came at his door.

Thinking it some drunken loafer, he made no reply till louder knocks and cries awakened him to get up since "the whole city is on fire and this building will be burnt in a few minutes." It was 2:00 A. M. he saw by the red and leaping light that shone in through the window. He raised the sash; "large and blazing coals" flew in and, slamming it down, he flew into his clothes and gathering important papers in his arms, fled to the street where men were howling, cursing and offering fabulous prices for drays to come and cart their belongings to safety.

Through the pandemonium he made his way to a bridge that would take him across toward the neighborhood where his daughter lay. It was afire. He tried another; it was burning, too. Sparks, raining down, burned the papers in his arms. Finally, by going south to Twelfth Street and circling west, he got behind the fire and saw that the flames were missing the region of the Shipman home. This fear allayed, he had time, as he walked toward the house, to eye "the grandeur of that immense sheet of

flame" which was eating out the heart of the downtown
section and in which, except for the night watchman, he
would have been destroyed. At 4:00 A. M. he burst in at
Dr. Shipman's door and caught his daughter in his arms.
She had been staring through the window at the inferno
and sobbing as she pictured her father dying in its midst.

His child relieved, Wright spent the rest of the night
in a kind of ecstacy; the mood of the Book of Revelations
was on him, in the red heavens a great bird was winging
—the Phoenix.

"With what power and gratitude my head and heart
worked upon the future of our city," he wrote his son
Augustine two days later, in describing the horrors and
rapture of that night. He had seen enough and reports
had come fast enough during the night to make it certain
the loss of life would be comparatively little. That settled,
nothing but sweeping good could result—slums gone, acres
of those hastily-made "balloon" buildings wiped out, the
decrepit past wiped away, room made for buildings worthy
of the city of his dreams—here was the chance for the new
city to build on a modern plan!

In recent years, Wright had intensified his study of
the Bible, and his letters to his children had been increas-
ingly devoted to religion and God's fulfillment of old Testament promises. Here in the fire was a new Manifestation!

Early the next morning while ruined men poked in the
hot wreckage of their buildings and United States troops
and police fired on ghoulish robbers and desolation was on
every face, John S. Wright came walking through the
ashes like a man through a garden on a morning in June.
At Wabash and Congress, someone called his name. It
was D. H. Horton, one of the publishers of his "Chicago;
Past, Present and Future," who now sneered:

"Well, Wright, what do you think *now* of the future of
Chicago?"

Wright thought for a moment, then replied, "I will tell you what it is, Horton. Chicago will have more men, more money, more business within five years than she would have had without this fire."[1]

Quickly the strange statement was passed through the crowds on the streets, old-timers explaining to newcomers that it had been said by a man who had always been a little crazy anyway.

The slogan burned like a gospel in Wright's mind. By the 24th of October he was in Boston trying to get close enough to capitalists to pour it into their ears. Renting a small room for $4 a week he spent his days haunting the anterooms of rich men. On Sundays he went to church and thought the clergymen preaching directly to him. On October 29, remembering that this was the thirty-ninth anniversary of his arrival in Chicago, he wrote to his sons that his boyhood removal from Massachusetts to Chicago would yet be seen by his wife and children to have been "for their best good, for time and eternity." Noble plans for rebuilding the schools and churches of his stricken city went thrillingly through his mind.

In his room he wrote a circular headed, "The Chicago Fire Will Help Wright's Washington Heights' Enterprise —A Grand Chance to Make Money and Help Chicago!"

Its first paragraph read:

" 'Five years will give Chicago more men, more money, more business, than she would have had without this fire.' While yet the sea of fire rolled in mastery over the doomed City, the above prediction was made by one who helped to raise the third frame building in 1833."

Laborers, men of wealth, Europeans would, he declared, now "see their opportunity of a life-time to gain position in this prostration of old establishments." The fire would give Chicago the chance to so equip herself with new build-

(1) "In Memoriam; John S. Wright," by Augustine W. Wright.

ings and factories and offices that she could meet the commercial demands of "The Great Interior" as she had never been able to do.

"Chicago is not burnt up, only well blistered for bad ailments, to strengthen her for manhood," he wrote, mixing his sexes recklessly in his excitement. "Nothing of the least consequence to the future of the city perished in the flames; only buildings and perishable property to be at once better replaced." The total value of the destroyed property would "only amount to about two years of average increase in the past eleven years."

The greatest single benefit from the fire, as he saw it, would be that Chicago would now do what no other city had had a chance to do, accommodate itself to the new phenomenon—the railroad. Chicago could now introduce sunken tracks for the locomotives, "leaving the streets above for ordinary use, with no danger to life and limb from locomotives and cars, where now over 30 are killed annually and many injured . . . this alone will pay over and over again the entire cost of this fire."

He told the East that its capitalists in the past had used Chicago for their own advantage, it was now their duty as well as their opportunity for greater profits to finance the immediate rebuilding of the town.

Into the circular he poured the last of his brave optimism; it carried the final flame of that prophetic fire which had burned in him for almost 40 years. Scattered over Boston and the East, it helped launch the flood of capital which rebuilt Chicago with startling rapidity, but it brought no aid to Wright's own projects. Investors, shrinking from the light that was in his eyes and the wildness that was in his voice, wouldn't entrust their money to him even though they agreed with everything he said about the opportunity.

Soon after Christmas in 1871, his wife and son Augustine were summoned to Boston in haste. Wright had been placed in an asylum for the insane. By January 15, they had calmed him and had moved him to a private home, where he wrote his son Chester, at Aberdeen, Arkansas, that he was thanking Father Almighty for freedom, "I believe we shall soon be brought together again in a family united in love and confidence as never hitherto." He saw prosperity only a little way ahead.

In the spring, when his wife and son had returned to Chicago, he was haunting the offices of wealthy New Yorkers again, finding them too busy to see him. Of evenings he wrote his children long letters about God, reminding them "religion is the controlling element in my character. Most earnestly have I prayed that I might not have success unless my children used the wealth well."

Refusing to come home, as his family wished, he wandered Boston like a mad preacher in a wilderness, his eyes and thoughts turning more each day to the Promised City beyond this life. Back home his daughter Maria, still ailing, was sent to friends in Denver, and his wife went to live for a time with his son Chester in Missouri. The older son Augustine, working with railroad builders at Helena, Arkansas, and married now, wrote Chester on May 13, 1872, to always remember how devoted their mother had been, and how much she had suffered "in changing from affluence to poverty . . . and if she should be impatient, bear with her infirmity. She wore out mentally and physically by her constant attendance upon our dear Father whose stay will I fear not be long upon this earth."

Late that summer, Wright was prevailed upon to return to Chicago where he was arrested and taken to the Insane Asylum at Elgin, nearby. He blamed his "cursed brothers" and vowed vengeance as soon as release could come. He looked at the other inmates and thought them the Apostles and Patriarchs. On October 27 he wrote Chester that "it is vastly more a shame to Chicago than to me . . . that I am kept here." In December he was strong enough to start writing a new circular appealing to the nation to adopt, on July Fourth, 1876, the Laws of Nature and Nature's God to replace the common law. This would ease the path of Man in the glorious years to come.

The future, the future, always the future!

His wife, working tirelessly, forced open the asylum doors in March and took Wright to that never-failing sanctuary—Hiram Kennicott's "Folly". Soon he opened offices at 397 Randolph Street in Chicago, and set about trying to recover some of the property he had assigned to his brothers in 1857. Two prominent lawyers took his case and assured him that under the bankrupt law his property had been so mishandled that he could recover 400 acres in Hyde Park, worth $1,000 an acre.

"Your mother is doing her best to make me happy," he wrote Chester on April 9, 1873, "and controls herself as never before. This is the best of earthly blessings and would make me happy, were I not so sure that Father Almighty is about to repeat in my case, the blessing of Job, after 40 years of trials. What were Job's trials to mine, except as to children."

Another panic was on the country when, in 1874, his family placed Wright in an asylum in Philadelphia, and another chill like that of 1837 was paralyzing the Eastern capitalists when on September 26, he died. His son, Augustine, weeping so hard he scarcely knew where his pen wandered, wrote Chester from Philadelphia, two days later, "All the Doctors agreed that Father's mind would never return. . . . It is better, far better as it is, but it is hard, so hard to part with him. I will send you a lock of his hair."

At the funeral in Chicago on October 1, one of the pallbearers was Philo Carpenter, remembering as he took hold of the coffin handle how he and Wright as boys had carried the surveyor's instrument out over that distant swamp land that was now deep in the city. Hiram Kennicott had hold of another of the silver handles as the casket went to its grave in Rosehill Cemetery. And at another handle marched William Bross, with the prophetic mantle of his master now his and his alone.

Bross had written for the *Tribune* the obituary which recorded the close of "one of the most useful lives ever passed in Chicago." Writing that, he had looked out upon a prairie which the New England emigrants, with Wright as their voice, had done so much to revolutionize. The open range had gone, green hedges fenced in blooded livestock, and the wire fence with barbs on it had just come—springing into being like the Osage Orange on the prairie, first of all. That same year of Wright's passing, the old law of the cattle-man was changed for good and all in Illinois—the law was at last as Wright had wanted it—favoring the little man, the grain grower, the one who lived the democratic life. The railroads for which he had pleaded till sound businessmen called him crazy—they filled his beloved city with a clangor that was the requiem Wright would have wanted. The little mud-town where he, as a boy, had counted 300 citizens, was now crowding the 400,000 mark and was fourth in the nation. His State, for which he had beat the tom-toms when it held only 475,000, was now past 2,750,000 in population, standing fourth among the commonwealths. The dairy cows were in the fields, the boulevards and parks were around Chicago, the meat-packers were leading the world, the Normal School was turning out teachers, the State Industrial University was welcoming farmers' sons.

There was another panic on the nation, and John Stephen Wright was no longer there to seize his pen and cry to the world that now was the time to invest in Chicago. But Deacon Bross was there. From Wright's grave, Bross, the new editor-in-charge-of-Chicago's-future, went to his desk and trumpeted forth the old rallying call. This newest panic, he cried, was only one more blessing to Chicago, for now anybody, everybody could see that the city was suffering far, far less than any other town in the land. Chicago had put its trust in livestock and grain, not in corporation stocks and bonds. It would come through this and all other depressions better than any of its rivals because it had hitched its future, long ago, to the star of the prairies.

THE END